Computer Science Illuminated

SECOND EDITION

NELL DALE
University of Texas, Austin

JOHN LEWIS
Villanova University

JONES AND BARTLETT PUBLISHERS

Sudbury, Massachusetts

BOSTON   TORONTO   LONDON   SINGAPORE

World Headquarters
Jones and Bartlett Publishers
40 Tall Pine Drive
Sudbury MA 01776
978-443-5000
info@jbpub.com
www.jbpub.com

Jones and Bartlett Publishers Canada
2406 Nikanna Road
Mississauga, ON L5C 2W6
CANADA

Jones and Bartlett Publishers International
Barb House, Barb Mews
London W6 7PA
UK

Copyright © 2004 by Jones and Bartlett Publishers, Inc.

ISBN: 0-7637-2624-9

Printed in the United States of America
07 06 05   10 9 8 7 6 5 4

Contents

How This Book Can Help You Learn Computer Science

All of us have different learning styles. Some of us are visual learners, some more auditory, some learn better by doing an activity. Some students prefer to learn new material using visual aids. Some learn material better when they hear it in a lecture; others learn it better by reading it. Cognitive research has shown that no matter what your learning style, you will learn more if you are actively engaged in the learning process.

The Student Lecture Companion will help you learn by providing a structure to your notes and letting you utilize all of the learning styles mentioned above. Students don't need to copy down every word their professor says or recopy their entire textbook. Do the assigned reading, listen in lecture, follow the key points your instructor is making, and write down meaningful notes. After reading and lectures, review your notes and pull out the most important points.

The Student Lecture Companion is your partner and guide in note-taking. Your Companion provides you with a visual guide that follows the chapter topics presented in your textbook, *Computer Science Illuminated, Second Edition*. The main topics covered in the lectures are listed in the Table of Contents. No more skimming through chapter after chapter trying to find the term you need to understand! If your instructor is using the PowerPoint slides that accompany the text, this guide will save you from having to write down everything that is on the slides. There is space provided for you to jot down the terms and concepts that you feel are most important to each lecture. By working with your Companion, you are seeing, hearing, writing, and, later, reading and reviewing. The more times you are exposed to the material, the better you will learn and understand it. Using different methods of exposure significantly increases your comprehension.

Your Companion is the perfect place to write down questions that you want to ask your professor later, interesting ideas that you want to discuss with your study group, or reminders to yourself to go back and study a certain concept again to make sure that you really got it.

Having organized notes is essential at exam time or when doing homework assignments. Your ability to easily locate the important concepts of a recent lecture will help you move along more rapidly, as you don't have to spend time rereading an entire chapter just to reinforce one point that you may not have quite understood.

Your Companion is a valuable resource. You've found a wonderful study partner!

Note-Taking Tips

1. It is easier to take notes if you are not hearing the information for the first time. Read the chapter or the material that is about to be discussed before class. This will help you to anticipate what will be said in class, and to have an idea of what to write down. It will also help to read over your notes from the last class. This way you can avoid having to spend the first few minutes of class trying to remember where you left off last time.

2. Don't waste your time trying to write down everything that your professor says. Instead, listen closely and write down only the important points. Review these important points after class to help remind you of related points that were made during the lecture.

3. If the class discussion takes a spontaneous turn, pay attention and participate in the discussion. Only take notes on the conclusions that are relevant to the lecture.

4. Emphasize main points in your notes. You may want to use a highlighter, special notation (asterisks, exclamation points), format (circle, underline), or placement on the page (indented, bulleted). You will find that when you try to recall these points, you will be able to actually picture them on the page.

5. Hearing something repeated, stressed, or summed up can be a signal that it is an important concept to understand.

6. Organize handouts, study guides, and exams in your notebook along with your lecture notes. It may be helpful to use a three-ring binder, so that you can insert pages wherever you need to.

7. When taking notes, you might find it helpful to leave a wide margin on all four sides of the page. Doing this allows you to note names, dates, definitions, etc. for easy access and studying later. It may also be helpful to make notes of questions you want to ask your professor about or research later, ideas or relationships that you want explore more on your own, or concepts that you don't fully understand.

8. It is best to maintain a separate notebook for each class. Labeling and dating your notes can be helpful when you need to look up information from previous lectures.

9. Make your notes legible, and take notes directly in your notebook. Chances are you won't recopy them no matter how noble your intentions. Spend the time you would have spent recopying the notes studying them instead, drawing conclusions and making connections that you didn't have time for in class.

10. Look over your notes after class while the lecture is still fresh in your mind. Fix illegible items and clarify anything you don't understand. Do this again right before the next class.

Key Terms

Absolute path A path that begins at the root and includes all successive subdirectories

Abstract data type A class of data objects with a defined set of properties and a set of operations that process the data objects while maintaining the properties; also called ADT

Abstract step An algorithmic step for which some details remain unspecified

Abstraction A mental model that removes complex details; a model of a complex system that includes only the details essential to the viewer; the separation of the logical properties of data or actions from their implementation details; the separation of the logical properties of an object from its implementation; (in OOD) the essential characteristics of an object from the viewpoint of the user

Access control policy A set of rules established by an organization that specify what types of network communication are permitted and denied

Access time The time it takes for a block to start being read; the sum of seek time and latency

Adder An electronic circuit that performs an addition operation on binary values

Addressability The number of bits stored in each addressable location in memory

Address binding The mapping from a logical address to a physical address

Aggregate operation An operation on a data structure as a whole, as opposed to an operation on an individual component of the data structure

Algorithm Unambiguous instructions for solving a problem or subproblem in a finite amount of time using a finite amount of data

Allocate To assign memory space at run time for use by an object

ALU See arithmetic/logic unit

Analog data Information represented in a continuous form

Application software Programs that help us solve real-world problems

Arguments The identifiers listed in parentheses on the subprogram call; sometimes called actual parameters

Arithmetic/logic unit The computer component that performs arithmetic operations (addition, subtraction, multiplication, division) and logical operations (comparison of two values)

Array A collection of components, all of the same type, ordered on n dimensions ($n \geq 1$); each component is accessed by n indices, each of which represents the component's position within that dimension

Artificial intelligence (AI) The study of computer systems that model and apply the intelligence of the human mind

Artificial neural network A computer representation of knowledge that attempts to mimic the neural networks of the human body

Assembler A program that translates an assembly-language program into machine code

Assembly language A low-level programming language in which a mnemonic represents each of the machine-language instructions for a particular computer

Assertion A logical proposition that is either true or false

Assignment statement A statement that stores the value of an expression into a variable

Asynchronous Not occurring at the same moment as some specific operation of the computer; in other words, not synchronized with the program's actions

Atomic data type A data type that allows only a single value to be associated with an identifier of that type

Attribute Part of a tag that provides additional information about the element

Auxiliary storage device A device that stores data in encoded form outside the computer's memory

Bandwidth The number of bits or bytes that can be transmitted from one place to another in a fixed amount of time

Base The foundational value of a number system, which dictates the number of digits and the value of digit positions

Base address The memory address of the first element of an array

Base case The case in a recursive solution for which the solution can be stated nonrecursively

Base class The class being inherited from

Base register A register that holds the beginning address of the current partition

Big-O notation A notation that expresses computing time (complexity) as the term in a function that increases most rapidly relative to the size of a problem

Binary digit A digit in the binary number system; a 0 or a 1

Binary file A file that contains data in a specific format, requiring a special interpretation of its bits

Binary operator An operator that has two operands

Binary search A search algorithm for sorted lists that involves dividing the list in half and determining, by value comparison, whether the item would be in the upper or lower half; the process is performed repeatedly until either the item is found or it is determined that the item is not on the list

Bit Short for binary digit

Block A group of zero or more statements enclosed in braces; the information stored in a sector on a disk

Body The statement(s) to be repeated within the loop; the executable statement(s) within a subprogram

Boolean algebra A mathematical notation for expressing two-value logical functions

Boolean expression A sequence of identifiers, separated by compatible operators, that evaluates to true or false

Boolean operators Operators applied to values of the type Boolean

Boolean type A data type consisting of only two values: true and false

Booting the system The process of starting up a computer by loading the operating system into its main memory

Bounds register A register that holds the length of the current partition

Brainstorming The beginning phase of an object-oriented design in which possible classes of objects in the problem are identified

Branch A code segment that is not always executed; for example, a switch or case statement has as many branches as there are case labels

Branching control structure See *selection control structure*

Breadth-first approach Searching across levels of a tree prior to searching down specific paths

Broadband Network technologies that generally provide data transfer speeds greater than 128 bps

Bus A set of wires that connect all major sections of a machine through which data flows

Bus topology A LAN configuration in which all nodes share a common line

Byte Eight binary digits

Bytecode A standard machine language into which Java source code is compiled

Cable modem A device that allows computer network communication using the cable TV hookup in a home

Call The point at which the computer begins following the instructions in a subprogram

Cancellation error A loss of accuracy during addition or subtraction of numbers of widely differing sizes, due to limits of precision

Cardinality constraint The number of relationships that may exist at one time between entities in an ER diagram

Case sensitive Uppercase and lowercase letters are not considered the same; two identifiers with the same spelling but different capitalization are considered to be two distinct identifiers

Cell An element of a spreadsheet that can contain data or a formula

Character set A list of the characters and the codes used to represent each one

Circuit A combination of interacting gates designed to accomplish a specific logical function

Circuit equivalence The same output for each corresponding input-value combination for two circuits

Circular reference A set of formulas that ultimately, and erroneously, rely on each other to compute their results

Class (general sense) A description of the behavior of a group of objects with similar properties and behaviors; (implementation phase) a pattern for an object

Class NP problems Problems that can be solved in polynomial time with as many processors as desired

Class P The class made up of all polynomial-time algorithms

Class P problems Problems that can be solved with one processor in polynomial time

Client Software that declares and manipulates objects of a particular class

Client/server model A distributed approach in which a client makes requests of a server and the server responds

Code Data type specifications and instructions for a computer that are written in a programming language

Code walk-through A verification process for a program in which each statement is examined to check that it faithfully implements the corresponding algorithmic step

Code-coverage (clear-box) testing Testing a program or subprogram based on covering all the statements in the code

Coding Translating an algorithm into a programming language; the process of assigning bit patterns to pieces of information

Collating sequence The ordering of the elements of a set or series, such as the characters (values) in a character set

Combinational circuit A circuit whose output is solely determined by its input values

Comment Explanatory text for the human reader

Compiler A program that translates a high-level language program into machine code

Complexity (of an algorithm) A measure of the effort expended by the computer in performing a computation, relative to the size of the computation

Composite data type A data type that allows a collection of values to be associated with an object of that type

Composition (containment) A mechanism by which an internal data member of one class is defined to be an object of another class type

Compression ratio The size of the compressed data divided by the size of the uncompressed data

Computer (electronic) A programmable device that can store, retrieve, and process data

Computer hardware The physical elements of a computing system

Computer network A collection of computing devices that are connected so that they can communicate and share resources

Computer program Data type specifications and instructions for carrying out operations that are used by a computer to solve a problem

Computer programming The process of specifying the data types and the operations for a computer to apply to data in order to solve a problem

Computer software The programs that provide the instructions that a computer executes

Computing system Computer hardware, software, and data, which interact to solve problems

Concrete step A step for which the details are fully specified

Conditional test The point at which the Boolean expression is evaluated and the decision is made to either begin a new iteration or skip to the first statement following the loop

Constant An item in a program whose value is fixed at compile time and cannot be changed during execution

Constant time An algorithm whose Big-O work expression is a constant

Constructor An operation that creates a new instance of a class; a method that has the same name as the class type containing it, which is called whenever an object of that type is instantiated

Container class A class into which you can add other elements

Containment A mechanism whereby one class contains an object of another class as a field

Context switch The exchange of register information that occurs when one process is removed from the CPU and another takes its place

Control abstraction The separation of the logical view of a control structure from its implementation

Control structure A statement used to alter the normally sequential flow of control; an instruction that determines the order in which other instructions in a program are executed

Control unit The computer component that controls the actions of the other components in order to execute instructions in sequence

Count-controlled loop A loop that executes a predetermined number of times

Counter A variable whose value is incremented to keep track of the number of times a process or event occurs

CPU A combination of the arithmetic/logic unit and the control unit; the "brain" of a computer that interprets and executes instructions

CPU scheduling The act of determining which process in memory is given access to the CPU so that it may execute

Crash The cessation of a computer's operations as a result of the failure of one of its components; cessation of program execution due to an error

CRC cards Index cards on which a class name is written along with its super- and sub-classes and a listing of the responsibilities and collaborators of the class; class, responsibility, collaboration

Cursor control keys A special set of keys on a computer keyboard that allow the user to move the cursor up, down, right, and left to any point on the screen

Cylinder The set of concentric tracks on all surfaces of a disk

Data Information in a form that a computer can use

Data abstraction The separation of the logical view of data from its implementation

Data compression Reducing the amount of space needed to store a piece of data

Data encapsulation The separation of the representation of data from the applications that use the data at a logical level; a programming language feature that enforces information hiding

Data representation The concrete form of data used to represent the abstract values of an abstract data type

Data structure A collection of data elements whose organization is characterized by accessing operations that are used to store and retrieve the individual data elements; the implementation of the composite data members in an abstract data type; the implementation of a composite data field in an abstract data type

Data transfer rate (also Bandwidth) The speed with which data is moved from one place to another on a network

Data type A description of the set of values and the basic set of operations that can be applied to values of the type

Data validation A test added to a program or a function that checks for errors in the data

Database management system A combination of software and data made up of the physical database, the database engine, and the database schema

Database A structured set of data

Data-coverage (black-box) testing Testing a program or subprogram based on the possible input values, treating the code as a black box

Deallocate To return the storage space for an object to the pool of free memory so that it can be reallocated to new objects

Debugging The process by which errors are removed from a program so that it does exactly what it is supposed to do

Declaration A statement that associates an identifier with a variable, an action, or some other entity within the language that can be given a name so that the programmer can refer to that item by name

Deep copy An operation that not only copies one class object to another but also makes copies of any pointed-to data

Demand paging An extension to paged memory management in which pages are brought into memory only when referenced (on demand)

Demotion (narrowing) The conversion of a value from a "higher" type to a "lower" type according to a programming language's precedence of data types; demotion may cause loss of information

Depth-first approach Searching down the paths of a tree prior to searching across levels

Derived class The class that inherits; a class that is created as an extension of another class in the hierarchy

Desk checking Tracing the execution of a design on paper

Development environment A single package containing all of the software required for developing a program

Dialog A style of user interface in which the user enters data and then performs a separate action (such as clicking a button) when the entered values are ready to be processed by the program

Digital data Information represented in a discrete form

Digital subscriber line (DSL) An Internet connection made using a digital signal on regular phone lines

Digitize The act of breaking down information into discrete pieces

Direct file access The technique in which data in a file is accessed directly by specifying logical record numbers

Directory A named group of files

Directory tree A structure showing the nested directory organization of the file system

Disk scheduling The act of deciding which outstanding requests for disk I/O to satisfy first

Documentation The written text and comments that make a program easier for others to understand, use, and modify

Document Type Definition (or DTD) A specification of the organization of an XML document

Domain name The part of a hostname that specifies a specific organization or group

Domain name server A computer that attempts to translate a hostname into an IP address

Domain name system A distributed system for managing hostname resolution

Down A descriptive term applied to a computer when it is not in a usable condition

Download Receiving data on your home computer from the Internet

Driver A simple dummy main program that is used to call a function being tested; a main function in an object-oriented program

Dumb terminal A monitor and keyboard that allow the user to access the mainframe computer in early timesharing systems

Dynamic allocation Allocation of memory space for a variable at run time (as opposed to static allocation at compile time)

Dynamic binding Determining at run time which form of a polymorphic method to call

Dynamic memory management The allocation and deallocation of storage space as needed while an application is executing

Dynamic-partition technique The memory management technique in which memory is divided into partitions as needed to accommodate programs

Echo printing Printing the data values input to a program to verify that they are correct

Editor An interactive program used to create and modify source programs or data

Effective weight In an artificial neuron, the sum of the weights multiplied by the corresponding input values

Encapsulation A language feature that enforces information hiding; bundling data and actions so that the logical properties of data and actions are separated from the implementation details

Entity-relationship (ER) modeling A popular technique for designing relational databases

ER diagram A graphical representation of an ER model

Ethernet The industry standard for local-area networks, based on a bus topology

Evaluate To compute a new value by performing a specified set of operations on given values

Event An action, such as a mouse click, that takes place asynchronously with respect to the execution of the program

Event counter A variable that is incremented each time a particular event occurs

Event handler A method that is part of an event listener and is invoked when the listener receives a corresponding event

Event handling The process of responding to events that can occur at any time during execution of the program

Event listener An object that is waiting for one or more events to occur

Event-controlled loop A loop that terminates when something happens inside the loop body to signal that the loop should be exited

Exception An unusual situation that is detected while a program is running; throwing an exception halts the normal execution of the method

Exception handler A section of a program that is executed when an exception occurs in Java or C++

Executing The action of a computer performing as instructed by a given program

Execution trace Going through the program with actual values recording the state of the variables

Expert system A software system based on the knowledge of human experts

Expression An arrangement of identifiers, literals, and operators that can be evaluated to compute a value of a given type

Expression statement A statement formed by appending a semicolon to an expression

Extensible Markup Language (or XML) A language that allows the user to describe the content of a document

Extensible Stylesheet Language (or XSL) A language for defining transformations from XML documents to other output formats

External file A file that is used to communicate with people or programs and is stored externally to the program

External pointer A named pointer variable that references the first node in a linked list

External representation The printable (character) form of a data value

Fetch-execute cycle The sequence of steps performed by the central processing unit for each machine-language instruction

Fields Named items in a class; can be data or subprograms

File A named collection of data, used for organizing secondary memory

File extension Part of a file name that indicates the file type

File server A computer dedicated to storing and managing files for network users

File system The operating system's logical view of the files it manages

File type The specific kind of information contained in a file, such as a Java program or a Microsoft Word document

Filtering The phase in an object-oriented design in which the proposed classes of objects from the brainstorming phase are refined and overlooked ones are added

Finite state machine An idealized model of a simple computer consisting of a set of states, the rules that specify when states are changed, and a set of actions that are performed when changing states

Firewall A gateway machine and its software that protect a network by filtering the traffic it allows

Firing an event An event source generates an event

Fixed-partition technique The memory management technique in which memory is divided into a specific number of partitions into which programs are loaded

Flag A Boolean variable that is set in one part of the program and tested in another to control the logical flow of a program

Floating point A representation of a real number that keeps track of the sign, mantissa, and exponent

Flow of control The order of execution of the statements in a program

Formatting The planned positioning of statements or declarations and blanks on a line of a program; the arranging of program output so that it is neatly spaced and aligned

Frame A fixed-size portion of main memory that holds a process page

Full adder A circuit that computes the sum of two bits, taking an input carry bit into account

Functional cohesion A property of a module in which all concrete steps are directed toward solving just one problem, and any significant subproblems are written as abstract steps

Functional decomposition A technique for developing software in which the problem is divided into more easily handled subproblems, the solutions of which create a solution to the overall problem; similar to top-down design.

Functional equivalence A property of a module that performs exactly the same operation as the abstract step it defines, or when one module performs exactly the same operation as another module

Functional modules In top-down design, the structured tasks and subtasks that are solved individually to create an effective program

Functional problem description A description that clearly states what a program is to do

Gate A device that performs a basic operation on electrical signals, accepting one or more input signals and producing a single output signal

Gateway A node that handles communication between its LAN and other networks

General (recursive) case The case in a recursive solution for which the solution is expressed in terms of a smaller version of itself

Half adder A circuit that computes the sum of two bits and produces the appropriate carry bit

Halting problem The unsolvable problem of determining if any program will eventually stop given particular input

Hardware The physical components of a computer

Heuristics Assorted problem-solving strategies

Hierarchy Structuring of abstractions in which a descendant object inherits the characteristics of its ancestors

High-level programming language Any programming language in which a single statement translates into one or more machine-language instructions

Homogeneous A descriptive term applied to structures in which all components are of the same data type (such as an array)

Host number The part of an IP address that specifies a particular host on the network

Hostname A name made up of words separated by dots that uniquely identifies a computer on the Internet; each hostname corresponds to a particular IP address

Huffman encoding Using a variable-length binary string to represent a character so that frequently used characters have short codes

Hypertext Markup Language (or HTML) The language used to create or build a web page

Identifier A name associated with a package, class, method, or field and used to refer to them

Implementation phase The second set of steps in programming a computer: translating (coding) the algorithm into a programming language; testing the resulting program by running it on a computer, checking for accuracy, and making any necessary corrections; using the program

Implementing Coding and testing an algorithm

Implementing a test plan Running the program with the test cases listed in the test plan

Index A value that selects a component of an array

Inference engine The software that processes rules to draw conclusions

Infinite loop A loop whose termination condition is never reached and therefore is never exited without intervention from outside of the program

Infinite recursion The situation in which a subprogram calls itself over and over continuously because a base case is never reached

Information Any knowledge that can be communicated

Information hiding The practice of hiding the details of a module with the goal of controlling access to the details of the module

Information system Software that helps the user organize and analyze data

Inheritance A mechanism by which one class acquires the properties—data fields and methods—of another class; a design technique used with a hierarchy of classes by which each descendant class inherits the properties (data and operations) of its ancestor class; a mechanism that enables us to define a new class by adapting the definition of an existing class

Input The process of placing values from an outside data set into variables in a program; the data may come from either an input device (keyboard) or an auxiliary storage device (disk or tape)

Input prompts Messages printed by an interactive program, explaining what data is to be entered

Input unit A device that accepts data to be stored in memory

Input/output (I/O) devices The parts of a computer that accept data to be processed (input) and present the results of that processing (output)

Inspection A verification method in which one member of a team reads the program or design line by line and the others point out errors

Instantiate To create an object from a class

Integer A natural number, a negative of a natural number, or zero

Integrated circuit (also **chip**) A piece of silicon on which multiple gates have been embedded

Interactive system A system that allows direct communication between the user and the computer

Internet A wide-area network that spans the planet

Internet backbone A set of high-speed networks carrying Internet traffic

Internet Protocol (IP) The network protocol that deals with the routing of packets through interconnected networks to the final destination

Internet service provider (ISP) A company providing access to the Internet

Interoperability The ability of software and hardware on multiple machines and from multiple commercial vendors to communicate

Interpreter A program that inputs a program in a high-level language and directs the computer to perform the actions specified in each statement

Invoke To call on a subprogram, causing the subprogram to execute before control is returned to the statement following the call

IP address An address made up of four numeric values separated by dots that uniquely identifies a computer on the Internet

Iteration An individual pass through, or repetition of, the body of a loop

Iteration counter A counter variable that is incremented with each iteration of a loop

Java applet A Java program designed to be embedded into an HTML document, transferred over the Web, and executed in a browser

JSP scriptlet A portion of code embedded in an HTML document designed to dynamically contribute to the content of the web page

Key One or more fields of a database record that uniquely identifies it among all other records in the table

Keyword encoding Substituting a frequently used word with a single character

Knowledge-based system Software that uses a specific set of information

Latency The time it takes for the specified sector to be in position under the read/write head

Length The number of items in a list; the length can vary over time

Lexical ambiguity The ambiguity created when words have multiple meanings

Lifetime For a variable, constant, or object, the portion of an application's execution time during which it is assigned storage space in the computer's memory

Linear relationship Each element except the first has a unique predecessor, and each element except the last has a unique successor

Linear time For an algorithm, when the Big-O work expression can be expressed in terms of a constant times n, where n is the number of values in a data set

Link A connection between one web page and another

Linked list A list in which the order of the components is determined by an explicit link field in each node, rather than by the sequential order of the components in memory

Literal value Any constant value written in a program

Loader A piece of software that takes a machine-language program and places it into memory

Local-area network (LAN) A network connecting a small number of nodes in a close geographic area

Loebner prize The first formal instantiation of the Turing test, held annually

Logarithmic order Algorithm complexity in which the Big-O work expression can be expressed in terms of the logarithm of n, where n is the number of values in a data set

Logging off Informing a computer—usually through a simple command—that no further commands follow

Logging on Taking the preliminary steps necessary to identify yourself to a computer so that it accepts your commands

Logic diagram A graphical representation of a circuit; each type of gate has its own symbol

Logical address A reference to a stored value relative to the program making the reference

Logical order The order in which the programmer wants the statements in the program to be executed, which may differ from the physical order in which they appear

Loop A method of structuring statements so that they are repeated while certain conditions are met

Loop entry The point at which the flow of control first passes to a statement inside a loop

Loop exit That point when the repetition of the loop body ends and control passes to the first statement following the loop

Loop test The point at which the loop expression is evaluated and the decision is made either to begin a new iteration or skip to the statement immediately following the loop

Lossless compression A technique in which there is no loss of information

Lossy compression A technique in which there is loss of information

Machine language The language made up of binary-coded instructions that is used directly by the computer

Mainframe A large, multi-user computer often associated with early timesharing systems

Maintenance The modification of a program, after it has been completed, in order to meet changing requirements or to take care of any errors that show up

Maintenance phase Period during which maintenance occurs

Mantissa With respect to floating-point representation of real numbers, the digits representing a number itself and not its exponent

Markup language A language that uses tags to annotate the information in a document

Memory management The act of keeping track of how and where programs are loaded in main memory

Memory unit Internal data storage in a computer

Metalanguage A language that is used to define other languages

Method A named algorithm that defines one aspect of the behavior of a class

Metropolitan-area network (MAN) A network infrastructure developed for a large city

MIME type A standard for defining the format of files that are included as email attachments or on websites

Model An abstraction of a real system; a representation of objects within a system and the rules that govern the behavior of the objects

Module A self-contained collection of steps that solves a problem or subproblem

Motherboard The main circuit board of a personal computer

Multimedia Several different media types

Multiplexer A circuit that uses a few input control signals to determine which of several input data lines is routed to its output

Multiprogramming The technique of keeping multiple programs in main memory at the same time, competing for the CPU

Named constant A location in memory, referenced by an identifier, that contains a data value that cannot be changed

Natural language Languages that human beings use to communicate, such as English

Natural language comprehension Using a computer to apply a meaningful interpretation to human communication

Natural number The number 0 and any number obtained by repeatedly adding 1 to it

Negative number A value less than 0, with a sign opposite to its positive counterpart

Nested control structure A program structure consisting of one control statement (selection, iteration, or subprogram) embedded within another control statement

Network address The part of an IP address that specifies a specific network

Node (or host) Any addressable device attached to a network

Nodes The building blocks of dynamic structures, each made up of a component (the data) and a pointer (the link) to the next node

Nonpreemptive scheduling CPU scheduling that occurs when the currently executing process gives up the CPU voluntarily

NP-complete problems A class of problems within Class NP that has the property that if a polynomial time solution with one processor can be found for any member of the class, such a solution exists for every member of the class

Number A unit of an abstract mathematical system subject to the laws of arithmetic

Object A collection of data values and associated operations

Object (problem-solving phase) An entity or thing that is relevant in the context of a problem

Object class or **Class** (problem-solving phase) A description of a group of objects with similar properties and behaviors

Object code A machine-language version of a source code

Object program The machine-language version of a source program

Object-based programming language A programming language that supports abstraction and encapsulation, but not inheritance

Object-oriented design A technique for developing software in which the solution is expressed in terms of objects--self-contained entities composed of data and operations on that data that interact by sending messages to one another

One-dimensional array A structured collection of components of the same type given a single name; each component is accessed by an index that indicates its position within the collection

Open system A system that is based on a common model of network architecture and an accompanying suite of protocols

Open Systems Interconnection Reference Model A seven-layer logical breakdown of network interaction to facilitate communication standards

Operating system System software that manages computer resources and provides an interface for system interaction

Out-of-bounds array index An index value that is less than the position of the first element or greater than the position of the last element

Output unit A device that prints or otherwise displays data stored in memory or makes a permanent copy of information stored in memory or another device

Overflow The condition that occurs when the results of a calculation are too large to represent in a given machine

Packet A unit of data sent across a network

Packet switching The approach to network communication in which packets are individually routed to their destination, then reassembled

Page A fixed-size portion of a process that is stored into a memory frame

Page map table (PMT) The table used by the operating system to keep track of page/frame relationships

Page swap Bringing in one page from secondary memory, possibly causing another to be removed

Paged memory technique A memory management technique in which processes are divided into fixed-size pages and stored in memory frames when loaded

Parameter The identifiers listed in parentheses beside the subprogram name; sometimes called formal parameters

Parameter list A mechanism for communicating between two parts of a program

Parameter passing The transfer of data between the arguments and parameters in a subprogram call

Pass by address A parameter-passing mechanism in which the memory address of the actual parameter is passed to the formal parameter; also called pass by reference

Pass by value A parameter-passing mechanism in which a copy of an actual parameter's value is passed to the formal parameter

Password A unique series of letters assigned to a user (and known only by that user) by which that user identifies himself or herself to a computer during the logging-on procedure; a password system protects information stored in a computer from being tampered with or destroyed

Path A text designation of the location of a file or subdirectory in a file system

Peripheral device An input, output, or auxiliary storage device attached to a computer

Personal computer (pc) A small computer system (usually intended to fit on a desktop) that is designed to be used primarily by a single person

Phone modem A device that converts computer data into an analog audio signal and back again

Phonemes The set of fundamental sounds made in any given natural language

Physical address An actual address in the main memory device

Ping A program used to test if a particular network computer is active and reachable

Pipelining processing Multiple processors arranged in tandem, where each contributes one part of an overall computation

Pixels Individual dots used to represent a picture; stands for picture elements

Polymorphism The ability of a language to have duplicate method names in an inheritance hierarchy and to apply the method that is appropriate for the object to which the method is applied

Polynomial-time algorithms Algorithms whose complexity can be expressed as a polynomial in the size of the problem

Port A numeric designation corresponding to a particular high-level protocol

Positional notation A system of expressing numbers in which the digits are arranged in succession, the position of each digit has a place value, and the number is equal to the sum of the products of each digit by its place value

Postfix operator An operator that follows its operand(s)

Precision The maximum number of significant digits that can be represented

Preconditions Assertions that must be true before a module begins execution

Preemptive scheduling CPU scheduling that occurs when the operating system decides to favor another process, preempting the currently executing process

Prefix operator An operator that precedes its operand(s)

Problem solving The act of finding a solution to a perplexing question

Problem-solving phase The first set of steps in programming a computer: analyzing the problem; developing an algorithm; testing the algorithm for accuracy

Procedural abstraction The separation of the logical view of an action from its implementation

Process The dynamic representation of a program during execution

Process control block (PCB) The data structure used by the operating system to manage information about a process

Process management The act of keeping track of information for active processes

Process states The conceptual stages through which a process moves as it is managed by the operating system

Program A sequence of instructions written to perform a specified task

Program counter (PC) The register that contains the address of the next instruction to be executed

Programming Planning, scheduling, or performing a task or an event; see also computer programming

Programming language A set of rules, symbols, and special words used to construct a program—that is, to express a sequence of instructions for a computer

Proprietary system A system that uses technologies kept private by a particular commercial vendor

Protocol A set of rules that define how data is formatted and processed on a network

Protocol stack Layers of protocols that build and rely on each other

Pseudocode A mixture of English statements and control structures that can easily be translated into a programming language

Pulse-code modulation Variation in a signal that jumps sharply between two extremes

Query A request for information submitted to a database

Radix point The dot that separates the whole part from the fractional part in a real number in any base

Range A set of contiguous cells specified by the endpoints

Range of values The interval within which values must fall, specified in terms of the largest and smallest allowable values

Raster-graphics format Storing image information pixel by pixel

Rational number An integer or the quotient of two integers (division by zero excluded)

Real number A number that has a whole and a fractional part and no imaginary part

Real-time system A system in which response time is crucial given the nature of the application domain

Reclock The act of reasserting an original digital signal before too much degradation occurs

Record (or object, or entity) A collection of related fields that make up a single database entry

Recursion The ability of a subprogram to call itself

Recursive call A subprogram call in which the subprogram being called is the same as the one making the call

Recursive case See *general case*

Recursive definition A definition in which something is defined in terms of a smaller version of itself

Reference parameter A parameter that expects the address of its argument to be passed by the calling unit (put on the message board)

Referential ambiguity The ambiguity created when pronouns could be applied to multiple objects

Refinement In top-down design, the expansion of a module specification to form a new module that solves a major step in the computer solution of a problem

Register A small storage area in the CPU used to store intermediate values or special data

Relational model A database model in which data and the relationships among them are organized into tables

Relational operators Operators that state that a relationship exists between two values

Relative path A path that begins at the current working directory

Repeater A network device that strengthens and propagates a signal along a long communication line

Representational (round-off) error An arithmetic error caused by the fact that the precision of the result of an arithmetic operation is greater than the precision of our machine

Reserved word A word in a language that has special meaning; it cannot be used as an identifier

Resolution The number of pixels used to represent a picture

Response time The time delay between receiving a stimulus and producing a response

Responsibility algorithms The algorithms for the class methods in an object-oriented design; the phase in the design process where the algorithms are developed

Return The point at which the computer comes back from executing a subprogram

Reuse The ability to use a class in any program without additional modification to either the class or the program

Right-justified Placed as far to the right as possible within a fixed number of character positions

Ring topology A LAN configuration in which all nodes are connected in a closed loop

Robust A descriptive term for a program that can recover from erroneous inputs and keep running

Root directory The topmost directory, in which all others are contained

Router A network device that directs a packet between networks toward its final destination

Rule-based system A software system based on a set of if-then rules

Run-length encoding Replacing a long series of a repeated characters with a count of the repetition

Scenarios The phase in an object-oriented design in which responsibilities are assigned to the classes

Schema A specification of the logical structure of data in a database

Scientific notation An alternative floating-point representation

Scope of access (scope) The region of program code where it is legal to reference (use) an identifier

Scope rules The rules that determine where in a program an identifier may be referenced, given the point where the identifier is declared and its specific access modifiers

Search tree A structure that represents alternatives in adversarial situations, such as game playing

Secondary storage device See auxiliary storage device

Sector A section of a track

Seek time The time it takes for the read/write head to get positioned over the specified track

Selection control structure A form of program structure allowing the computer to select one of several possible actions to perform based on given circumstances; also called a branching control structure

Self-documenting code A program containing meaningful identifiers as well as judiciously used clarifying comments

Semantic network A knowledge representation technique that represents the relationships among objects

Semantics The set of rules that gives the meaning of instructions in a language

Semiconductor Material such as silicon that is neither a good conductor nor insulator

Sentinel A special data value used in certain event-controlled loops as a signal that the loop should be exited

Sequence A structure in which statements are executed one after another

Sequential circuit A circuit whose output is a function of input values and the current state of the circuit

Sequential file access The technique in which data in a file is accessed in a linear fashion

Shallow copy An operation that copies one class object to another without copying any pointed-to data

Shared memory Multiple processors share a global memory

Short-circuit (conditional) evaluation Evaluation of a logical expression in left-to-right order with evaluation stopping as soon as the final boolean value can be determined

Significant digits Those digits that begin with the first nonzero digit on the left and end with the last nonzero digit on the right (or a zero digit that is exact)

Sign-magnitude representation Number representation in which the sign represents the ordering of the number (negative and positive) and the value represents the magnitude

Simulation Developing a model of a complex system and experimenting with the model to observe the results

Single contiguous memory management The approach to memory management in which a program is loaded into one continuous area of memory

Size (of an array) The physical space reserved for an array

Software Computer programs; the set of all programs available on a computer

Software engineering The application of traditional engineering methodologies and techniques to the development of software

Software life cycle The phases in the life of a large software project, including requirements analysis, specification, design, implementation, testing, and maintenance

Software piracy The unauthorized copying of software for either personal use or use by others

Software requirements A statement of what is to be provided by a computer system or software product

Software specification A detailed description of the function, inputs, processing, outputs, and special features of a software product; provides the information needed to design and implement the software

Sort key The field to be used in the ordering

Sorted list A list with predecessor and successor relationships determined by the content of the keys of the items in the list; there is a semantic relationship among the keys of the items in the list

Sorting Putting a list of items in order, either numerically or alphabetically

Source program A program written in a high-level programming language

Spatial compression Movie compression technique based on the same compression techniques used for still images

Spreadsheet A program that allows the user to organize and analyze data using a grid of cells

Spreadsheet function A computation provided by the spreadsheet software that can be incorporated into formulas

Stable sort A sorting algorithm that preserves the order of duplicates

Standardized Made uniform; most high-level languages are standardized, as official descriptions of them exist

Star topology A LAN configuration in which a central node controls all message traffic

String (general sense) A sequence of characters, such as a word, name, or sentence, enclosed in double quotes

Strong equivalence The equality of two systems based on their results and the process by which they arrive at those results

Strong typing Each variable is assigned a type, and only values of that type can be stored in the variable

Structured data type An organized collection of components; the organization determines the method used to access individual components

Structured Query Language (SQL) A comprehensive relational database language for data management and queries

Style The individual manner in which computer programmers translate algorithms into a programming language

Supercomputer The most powerful class of computers

Synchronous processing Multiple processors apply the same program in lockstep to multiple data sets

Syntactic ambiguity The ambiguity created when sentences can be constructed in various ways

Syntax The formal rules governing the construction of valid instructions

System software Programs that manage a computer system and interact with hardware

Table A collection of database records

Tag The syntactic element in a markup language that indicates how information should be displayed

Tail recursion A recursive algorithm in which no statements are executed after the return from the recursive call

TCP/IP A suite of protocols and programs that support low-level network communication

Team programming The use of two or more programmers to design a program that would take one programmer too long to complete

Temporal compression Movie compression technique based on differences between consecutive frames

Ten's complement A representation of negative numbers such that the negative of I is 10 raised to k minus I.

Termination condition The condition that causes a loop to be exited

Test plan A document that specifies how a program is to be tested

Testing Checking a program's output by comparing it to hand-calculated results; running a program with data sets designed to discover any errors

Test-plan implementation Using the test cases specified in a test plan to verify that a program outputs the predicted results

Text file A file that contains characters

Thrashing Inefficient processing caused by constant page swapping

Throw The act of signaling that an exception has occurred; throwing an exception abnormally terminates the execution of a subprogram

Time slice The amount of time given to each process in the round-robin CPU scheduling algorithm

Timesharing A system in which CPU time is shared among multiple interactive users at the same time

Top-down design A technique for developing a program in which the problem is divided into more easily handled subproblems, the solutions of which create a solution to the overall problem

Top-level domain (TLD) The last section of a domain name, specifying the type of organization or its country of origin

Traceroute A program that shows the route a packet takes across the Internet

Track A concentric circle on the surface of a disk

Training The process of adjusting the weights and threshold values in a neural net to get a desired outcome

Transfer rate The rate at which data moves from the disk to memory

Transistor A device that acts either as a wire or a resister, depending on the voltage level of an input signal

Transmission Control Protocol (TCP) The network protocol that breaks messages into packets, reassembles them at the destination, and takes care of errors

Traverse a list To access the components of a list one at a time from the beginning of the list to the end

Truth table A table showing all possible input values and the associated output values

Turing test A behavioral approach to determining whether a computer system is intelligent

Turnaround time The CPU scheduling metric that measures the elapsed time between a process's arrival in the ready state and its ultimate completion

Two-dimensional array A collection of components, all of the same type, structured in two dimensions; each component is accessed by a pair of indices that represent the component's position within each dimension

Type casting (type conversion) The explicit conversion of a value from one data type to another

Type coercion An automatic conversion of a value of one type to a value of another type

Unary operator An operator that has only one operand

Underflow The condition that occurs when the results of a calculation are too small to represent in a given machine

Uniform Resource Locator (or URL) A standard way of specifying the location of a web page

Unstructured data type A collection consisting of components that are not organized with respect to one another

Upload Sending data from your home computer to a destination on the Internet

User name The name by which a computer recognizes the user, and which must be entered to log on to a machine

User Datagram Protocol (UDP) An alternative to TCP that achieves higher transmission speeds at the cost of reliability

Value parameter A parameter that expects a copy of its argument to be passed by the calling unit (put on the message board)

Value-returning function A function (subprogram) that returns a single value to its caller and is invoked from within an expression

Variable A location in memory, referenced by an identifier, that contains a data value

Vector graphics Representation of an image in terms of lines and shapes

Video codec Methods used to shrink the size of a movie

Virtual computer (machine) A hypothetical machine designed to illustrate important features of a real machine

Virtual machine The illusion created by a timesharing system that each user has a dedicated machine; the illusion that there is no restriction on program size because an entire process need not be in memory at the same time

Virus A computer program that replicates itself, often with the goal of spreading to other computers without authorization, possibly with the intent of doing harm

Voice recognition Using a computer to recognize the words spoken by a human

Voice synthesis Using a computer to create the sound of human speech

Voiceprint The plot of frequency changes over time, representing the sound of human speech

Walk-through A verification method in which a team performs a manual simulation of the program or design

Weak equivalence The equality of two systems based on their results

Web browser A software tool that retrieves and displays web pages

Web page A document that contains or references various kinds of data

Web server A computer set up to respond to requests for web pages

Web site A collection of related web pages, usually designed and controlled by the same person or company

What-if analysis Modifying spreadsheet values that represent assumptions to see how changes in those assumptions affect related data

Wide-area network (WAN) A network connecting two or more local-area networks

Wireless A network connection made without physical wires

Word A group of one or more bytes; the number of bits in a word is the word length of the computer

Work A measure of the effort expended by the computer in performing a computation

Working directory The currently active subdirectory

Workstation A minicomputer or powerful microcomputer designed to be used primarily by one person at a time

World Wide Web (or Web) An infrastructure of information and the network software used to access it

Chapter 1: The Big Picture

Notes

Computer Science
Illuminated
SECOND EDITION
Nell Dale • John Lewis

Chapter 1

Chapter Goals

- Describe the layers of a computer system
- Describe the concept of abstraction and its relationship to computing
- Describe the history of computer hardware and software
- Describe the changing role of the computer user
- Distinguish between systems programmers and applications programmers
- Distinguish between computing as a tool and computing as a discipline

1-2

Computing Systems

Computing systems are dynamic!

*What is the difference between **hardware** and **software**?*

1-3

Notes

Computing Systems

Hardware The physical elements of a computing system (printer, circuit boards, wires, keyboard…)

Software The programs that provide the instructions for a computer to execute

1-4

Layers of a Computing System

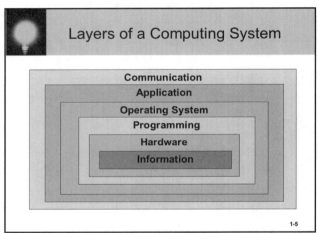

Communication
Application
Operating System
Programming
Hardware
Information

1-5

Abstraction

Abstraction A mental model that removes complex details

This is a key concept. Abstraction will reappear throughout the text – be sure to understand it!

1-6

Notes

Early History of Computing

Abacus
An early device to record numeric values

Blaise Pascal
Mechanical device to add, subtract, divide & multiply

Joseph Jacquard
Jacquard's Loom, the punched card

Charles Babbage
Analytical Engine

1-7

Early History of Computing

Ada Lovelace
First Programmer, the loop

Alan Turing
Turing Machine, Artificial Intelligence Testing

Harvard Mark I, ENIAC, UNIVAC I
Early computers launch new era in mathematics, physics, engineering and economics

1-8

First Generation Hardware (1951-1959)

Vacuum Tubes
Large, not very reliable, generated a lot of heat

Magnetic Drum
Memory device that rotated under a read/write head

Card Readers → Magnetic Tape Drives
Sequential auxiliary storage devices

1-9

Notes

Second Generation Hardware (1959-1965)

Transistor
Replaced vacuum tube, fast, small, durable, cheap

Magnetic Cores
Replaced magnetic drums, information available instantly

Magnetic Disks
Replaced magnetic tape, data can be accessed directly

1-10

Third Generation Hardware (1965-1971)

Integrated Circuits
Replaced circuit boards, smaller, cheaper, faster, more reliable.

Transistors
Now used for memory construction

Terminal
An input/output device with a keyboard and screen

1-11

Fourth Generation Hardware (1971-?)

Large-scale Integration
Great advances in chip technology

PCs, the Commercial Market, Workstations
Personal Computers were developed as new companies like Apple and Atari came into being. Workstations emerged.

1-12

Parallel Computing and Networking

Parallel Computing
Computers rely on interconnected central processing units that increase processing speed.

Networking
With the Ethernet small computers could be connected and share resources. A file server connected PCs in the late 1980s.

ARPANET and LANs → Internet

1-13

First Generation Software (1951-1959)

Machine Language
Computer programs were written in binary (1s and 0s)

Assembly Languages and translators
Programs were written in artificial programming languages and were then translated into machine language

Programmer Changes
Programmers divide into application programmers and systems programmers

1-14

Second Generation Software (1959-1965)

High Level Languages
Use English-like statements and make programming easier.
Fortran, COBOL, Lisp are examples.

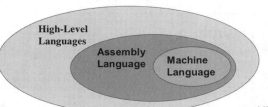

1-15

Third Generation Software (1965-1971)

- **Systems Software**
  - utility programs,
  - language translators,
  - and the operating system, which decides which programs to run and when.
- **Separation between Users and Hardware**
  Computer programmers began to write programs to be used by people who did not know how to program

1-16

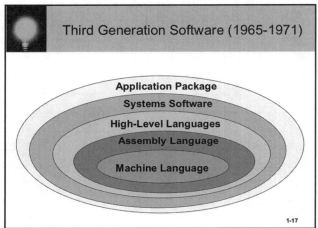

Third Generation Software (1965-1971)

Application Package
Systems Software
High-Level Languages
Assembly Language
Machine Language

1-17

Fourth Generation Software (1971-1989)

Structured Programming
Pascal, C, C++

New Application Software for Users
Spreadsheets, word processors, database management systems

1-18

Fifth Generation Software (1990- present)

Microsoft
The Windows operating system, and other Microsoft application programs dominate the market

Object-Oriented Design
Based on a hierarchy of data objects (i.e. Java)

World Wide Web
Allows easy global communication through the Internet

New Users
Today's user needs no computer knowledge

1-19

Computing as a Tool

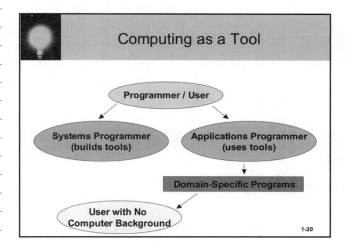

1-20

Computing as a Discipline

- ***What can be (efficiently) automated?***

- **Four Necessary Skills**
  1. Algorithmic Thinking
  2. Representation
  3. Programming
  4. Design

1-21

Computing as a Discipline

What do you think?

Is Computer Science a mathematical, scientific, or engineering discipline?

1-22

Systems Areas of Computer Science

- **Algorithms and Data Structures**
- **Programming Languages**
- **Architecture**
- **Operating Systems**
- **Software Methodology and Engineering**
- **Human-Computer Communication**

1-23

Application Areas of Computer Science

- **Numerical and Symbolic Computation**
- **Databases and Information Retrieval**
- **Artificial Intelligence and Robotics**
- **Graphics**
- **Organizational Informatics**
- **Bioinformatics**

1-24

Chapter 2: Binary Values and Number Systems

Notes

Computer Science Illuminated
SECOND EDITION
Nell Dale • John Lewis

Chapter 2

Chapter Goals

- Know the different types of numbers
- Describe positional notation
- Convert numbers in other bases to base 10
- Convert base 10 numbers into numbers of other bases
- Describe the relationship between bases 2, 8, and 16
- Explain computing and bases that are powers of 2

2-2

Numbers

Natural Numbers
Zero and any number obtained by repeatedly adding one to it.

Examples: 100, 0, 45645, 32

Negative Numbers
A value less than 0, with a – sign

Examples: -24, -1, -45645, -32

2-3

Notes

Numbers

Integers
A natural number, a negative number, zero

Examples: 249, 0, - 45645, - 32

Rational Numbers
An integer or the quotient of two integers

Examples: -249, -1, 0, 3/7, -2/5

2-4

Natural Numbers

How many ones are there in 642?

600 + 40 + 2 ?
Or is it
384 + 32 + 2 ?
Or maybe…
1536 + 64 + 2 ?

2-5

Natural Numbers

Aha!

642 is 600 + 40 + 2 in **BASE 10**

The **base** of a number determines the number of digits and the value of digit positions

2-6

Notes

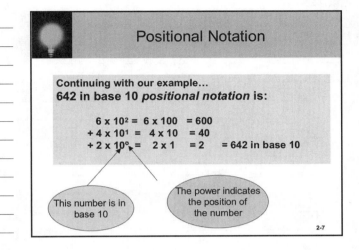

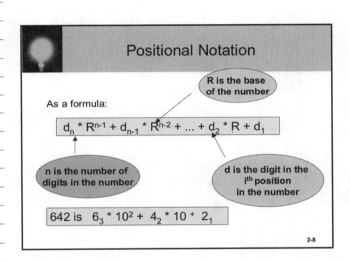

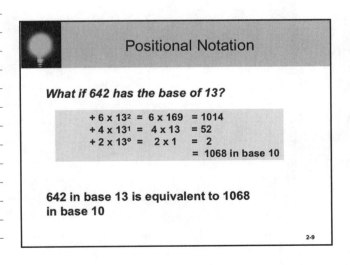

Notes

Binary

Decimal is base 10 and has 10 digits:
0,1,2,3,4,5,6,7,8,9

Binary is base 2 and has 2 digits:
0,1

For a number to exist in a given number system, the number system must include those digits. For example, the number 284 only exists in base 9 and higher.

2-10

Bases Higher than 10

How are digits in bases higher than 10 represented?

With distinct symbols for 10 and above.

Base 16 has 16 digits:
0,1,2,3,4,5,6,7,8,9,A,B,C,D,E, and F

2-11

Converting Octal to Decimal

What is the decimal equivalent of the octal number 642?

$$6 \times 8^2 = 6 \times 64 = 384$$
$$+ 4 \times 8^1 = 4 \times 8 = 32$$
$$+ 2 \times 8^0 = 2 \times 1 = 2$$
$$= 418 \text{ in base 10}$$

2-12

Converting Hexadecimal to Decimal

What is the decimal equivalent of the hexadecimal number DEF?

$$
\begin{aligned}
D \times 16^2 &= 13 \times 256 = 3328 \\
+ E \times 16^1 &= 14 \times 16 = 224 \\
+ F \times 16^0 &= 15 \times 1 \;\;= 15 \\
&= 3567 \text{ in base 10}
\end{aligned}
$$

Remember, the digits in base 16 are
0,1,2,3,4,5,6,7,8,9,A,B,C,D,E,F

2-13

Converting Binary to Decimal

What is the decimal equivalent of the binary number 1101110?

$$
\begin{aligned}
1 \times 2^6 &= 1 \times 64 = 64 \\
+ 1 \times 2^5 &= 1 \times 32 = 32 \\
+ 0 \times 2^4 &= 0 \times 16 = 0 \\
+ 1 \times 2^3 &= 1 \times 8 = 8 \\
+ 1 \times 2^2 &= 1 \times 4 = 4 \\
+ 1 \times 2^1 &= 1 \times 2 = 2 \\
+ 0 \times 2^0 &= 0 \times 1 = 0 \\
&= 110 \text{ in base 10}
\end{aligned}
$$

2-14

Arithmetic in Binary

Remember that there are only 2 digits in binary, 0 and 1

Position is key, carry values are used:

```
  1 1 1 1 1 1        ← Carry Values
  1 0 1 0 1 1 1
+ 1 0 0 1 0 1 1
-------------
1 0 1 0 0 0 1 0
```

2-15

Notes

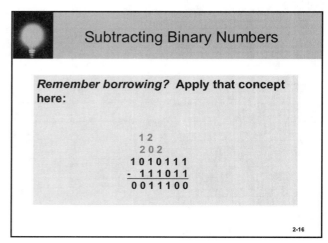

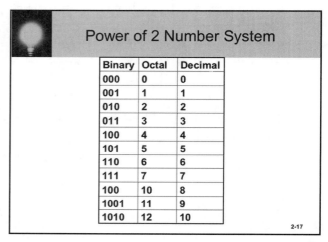

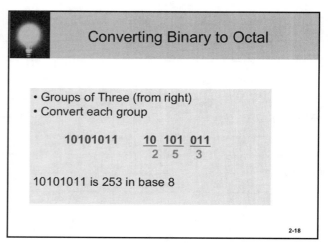

Notes

Converting Binary to Hexadecimal

- Groups of Four (from right)
- Convert each group

10101011   1010 1011
               A   B

10101011 is AB in base 16

2-19

Converting Decimal to Other Bases

Algorithm for converting base 10 to other bases

While the quotient is *not* zero

Divide the decimal number by the new base

Make the remainder the next digit to the left in the answer

Replace the original dividend with the quotient

2-20

Converting Decimal to Hexadecimal

Try a Conversion

The base 10 number 3567 is what number in base 16?

2-21

Notes

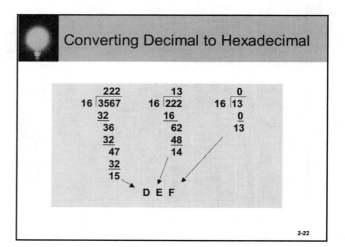

Converting Decimal to Hexadecimal

```
      222           13          0
  16 |3567      16 |222     16 |13
      32            16           0
      36            62          13
      32            48
      47            14
      32
      15
               D  E  F
```

2-22

Binary and Computers

Binary computers have storage units called binary digits or bits

Low Voltage = 0
High Voltage = 1   all bits have 0 or 1

2-23

Binary and Computers

Byte 8 bits

The number of bits in a word determines the word length of the computer, but it is usually a multiple of 8

- 32-bit machines
- 64-bit machines etc.

2-24

Chapter 3: Data Representation

Notes

Computer Science Illuminated
SECOND EDITION
Nell Dale • John Lewis

Chapter 3

Chapter Goals

- Distinguish between analog and digital information.
- Explain data compression and calculate compression ratios.
- Explain the binary formats for negative and floating-point values.
- Describe the characteristics of the ASCII and Unicode character sets.

3-2

Chapter Goals

- Perform various types of text compression.
- Explain the nature of sound and its representation.
- Explain how RGB values define a color.
- Distinguish between raster and vector graphics.
- Explain temporal and spatial video compression.

3-3

Data and Computers

- Computers are **multimedia** devices, dealing with a vast array of information categories. Computers store, present, and help us modify
    - Numbers
    - Text
    - Audio
    - Images and graphics
    - Video

3-4

Data and Computers

- **Data compression** Reduction in the amount of space needed to store a piece of data.
- **Compression ratio** The size of the compressed data divided by the size of the original data.
- A data compression techniques can be
    - **lossless**, which means the data can be retrieved without any loss of the original information,
    - **lossy**, which means some information may be lost in the process of compaction.

3-5

Analog and Digital Information

- Computers are finite. Computer memory and other hardware devices have only so much room to store and manipulate a certain amount of data. The goal, is to represent enough of the world to satisfy our computational needs and our senses of sight and sound.

3-6

Notes

Analog and Digital Information

- Information can be represented in one of two ways: **analog** or **digital**.

    Analog data A continuous representation, analogous to the actual information it represents.

    Digital data A discrete representation, breaking the information up into separate elements.

    A mercury thermometer is an analog device. The mercury rises in a continuous flow in the tube in direct proportion to the temperature.

3-7

Analog and Digital Information

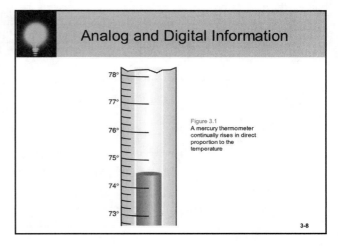

Figure 3.1
A mercury thermometer continually rises in direct proportion to the temperature

3-8

Analog and Digital Information

- Computers, cannot work well with analog information. So we **digitize** information by breaking it into pieces and representing those pieces separately.
- *Why do we use binary?* Modern computers are designed to use and manage binary values because the devices that store and manage the data are far less expensive and far more reliable if they only have to represent on of two possible values.

3-9

Notes

Electronic Signals

- An analog signal continually fluctuates in voltage up and down. But a digital signal has only a high or low state, corresponding to the two binary digits.
- All electronic signals (both analog and digital) degrade as they move down a line. That is, the voltage of the signal fluctuates due to environmental effects.

3-10

Electronic Signals *(Cont'd)*

- Periodically, a digital signal is **reclocked** to regain its original shape.

Figure 3.2
An analog and a digital signal

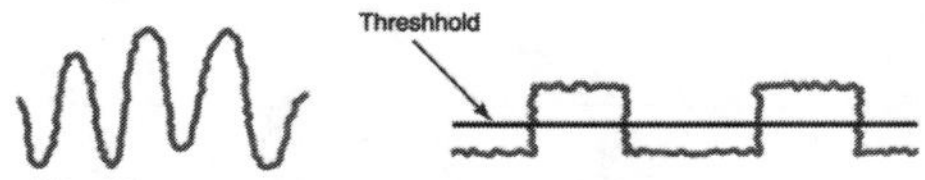

Threshhold

Figure 3.3
Degradation of analog and digital signals

3-11

Binary Representations

- One bit can be either 0 or 1. Therefore, one bit can represent only two things.
- To represent more than two things, we need multiple bits. Two bits can represent four things because there are four combinations of 0 and 1 that can be made from two bits: 00, 01, 10,11.

3-12

Notes

_____

_____

_____

_____

_____

_____

_____

_____

_____

_____

_____

_____

_____

_____

_____

_____

_____

_____

_____

_____

_____

_____

_____

_____

_____

_____

_____

_____

_____

_____

_____

_____

_____

_____

_____

_____

_____

Binary Representations

- If we want to represent more than four things, we need more than two bits. Three bits can represent eight things because there are eight combinations of 0 and 1 that can be made from three bits.

3-13

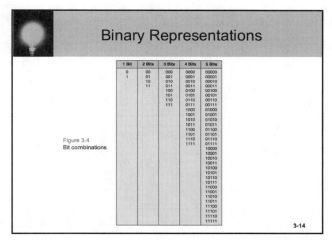

Binary Representations

Figure 3.4
Bit combinations

1 Bit	2 Bits	3 Bits	4 Bits	5 Bits
0	00	000	0000	00000
1	01	001	0001	00001
	10	010	0010	00010
	11	011	0011	00011
		100	0100	00100
		101	0101	00101
		110	0110	00110
		111	0111	00111
			1000	01000
			1001	01001
			1010	01010
			1011	01011
			1100	01100
			1101	01101
			1110	01110
			1111	01111
				10000
				10001
				10010
				10011
				10100
				10101
				10110
				10111
				11000
				11001
				11010
				11011
				11100
				11101
				11110
				11111

3-14

Binary Representations

- In general, n bits can represent 2^n things because there are 2^n combinations of 0 and 1 that can be made from n bits. Note that every time we increase the number of bits by 1, we double the number of things we can represent.

3-15

Notes

Representing Negative Values

- You have used the **signed-magnitude representation** of numbers since grade school. The sign represents the ordering, and the digits represent the magnitude of the number.

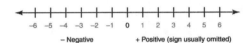

– Negative   + Positive (sign usually omitted)

3-16

Representing Negative Values

- There is a problem with the sign-magnitude representation.

  There are two representations of zero. There is plus zero and minus zero. Two representations of zero within a computer can cause unnecessary complexity. If we allow only a fixed number of values, we can represent numbers as just integer values, where half of them represent negative numbers.

3-17

Representing Negative Values

- For example, if the maximum number of decimal digits we can represent is two, we can let 1 through 49 be the positive numbers 1 through 49 and let 50 through 99 represent the negative numbers -50 through -1.

3-18

Notes

Representing Negative Values

- To perform addition within this scheme, you just add the numbers together and discard any carry.

Sign-Magnitude	New Scheme
5 + − 6 − 1	5 + 94 99
− 4 + 6 2	96 + 6 2
− 2 + − 4 − 6	98 + 96 94

3-19

Representing Negative Values

- A-B=A+(-B). We can subtract one number from another by adding the negative of the second to the first.

Sign – Magnitude	New Scheme	Add Negative
−5 − 3 −8	95 − 3	95 + 97 92

3-20

Representing Negative Values

- Here is a formula that you can use to compute the negative representation

$Negative(I) = 10^k - I$, where k is the number of digits

- This representation of negative numbers is called the **ten's complement.**

3-21

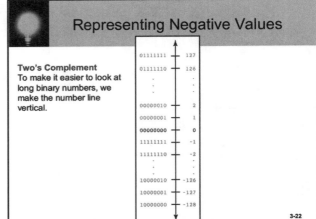

Representing Negative Values

Two's Complement
To make it easier to look at long binary numbers, we make the number line vertical.

```
01111111  ──┬── 127
01111110  ──┼── 126
      .     ·    .
      .     ·    .
      .     ·    .
00000010  ──┼── 2
00000001  ──┼── 1
00000000  ──┼── 0
11111111  ──┼── -1
11111110  ──┼── -2
      .     ·    .
      .     ·    .
10000010  ──┼── -126
10000001  ──┼── -127
10000000  ──┼── -128
```

3-22

Representing Negative Values

- Addition and subtraction are accomplished the same way as in 10's complement arithmetic

```
-127  10000001
+      100000001
-126  10000010
```

- Notice that with this representation, the leftmost bit in a negative number is always a 1.

3-23

Number Overflow

- **Overflow** occurs when the value that we compute cannot fit into the number of bits we have allocated for the result. For example, if each value is stored using eight bits, adding 127 to 3 overflows.

```
   1111111
+  0000011
  10000010
```

- Overflow is a classic example of the type of problems we encounter by mapping an infinite world onto a finite machine.

3-24

Notes

Representing Real Numbers

- Real numbers have a whole part and a fractional part. For example 104.32, 0.999999, 357.0, and 3.14159.
  - the digits represent values according to their position, and
  - those position values are relative to the base.
- The positions to the right of the decimal point are the tenths position (10^{-1} or one tenth), the hundredths position (10^{-2} or one hundredth), etc.

3-25

Representing Real Numbers

- In binary, the same rules apply but the base value is 2. Since we are not working in base 10, the decimal point is referred to as a **radix point**.
- The positions to the right of the radix point in binary are the halves position (2^{-1} or one half), the quarters position (2^{-2} or one quarter), etc.

3-26

Representing Real Numbers

- A real value in base 10 can be defined by the following formula.

$$sign * mantissa * 10^{exp}$$

- The representation is called **floating point** because the number of digits is fixed but the radix point floats.

3-27

Representing Real Numbers

Real Value	Floating-Point Value
12001.00	$12001*10^0$
−120.01	$−12001*10^{-2}$
0.12000	$12000*10^{-5}$
−123.10	$−12310*10^{-2}$
155555000.00	$15555*10^3$

- Likewise, a binary floating –point value is defined by the following formula:

$$sign * mantissa * 2^{exp}$$

3-28

Representing Real Numbers

- **Scientific notation** A form of floating-point representation in which the decimal point is kept to the right of the leftmost digit.

  For example, 12001.32708 would be written as 1.200132708E+4 in scientific notation.

3-29

Representing Text

- To represent a text document in digital form, we need to be able to represent every possible character that may appear.
- There are finite number of characters to represent, so the general approach is to list them all and assign each a binary string.
- A **character set** is a list of characters and the codes used to represent each one.
- By agreeing to use a particular character set, computer manufacturers have made the processing of text data easier.

3-30

Notes

The ASCII Character Set

- ASCII stands for American Standard Code for Information Interchange. The ASCII character set originally used seven bits to represent each character, allowing for 128 unique characters.
- Later ASCII evolved so that all eight bits were used which allows for 256 characters.

3-31

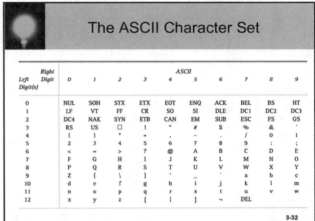

The ASCII Character Set

Left Digit(s)	Right Digit	0	1	2	3	4	5	6	7	8	9
						ASCII					
0		NUL	SOH	STX	ETX	EOT	ENQ	ACK	BEL	BS	HT
1		LF	VT	FF	CR	SO	SI	DLE	DC1	DC2	DC3
2		DC4	NAK	SYN	ETB	CAN	EM	SUB	ESC	FS	GS
3		RS	US	□	!	"	#	$	%	&	'
4		(	)	*	+	,	-	.	/	0	1
5		2	3	4	5	6	7	8	9	:	;
6		<	=	>	?	@	A	B	C	D	E
7		F	G	H	I	J	K	L	M	N	O
8		P	Q	R	S	T	U	V	W	X	Y
9		Z	[	\	]	^	_	`	a	b	c
10		d	e	f	g	h	i	j	k	l	m
11		n	o	p	q	r	s	t	u	v	w
12		x	y	z	{	|	}	~	DEL		

3-32

The ASCII Character Set

- Note that the first 32 characters in the ASCII character chart do not have a simple character representation that you could print to the screen.

3-33

Notes

The Unicode Character Set

- The extended version of the ASCII character set is not enough for international use.
- The Unicode character set uses 16 bits per character. Therefore, the Unicode character set can represent 216, or over 65 thousand, characters.
- Unicode was designed to be a superset of ASCII. That is, the first 256 characters in the Unicode character set correspond exactly to the extended ASCII character set.

3-34

The Unicode Character Set

Code (Hex)	Character	Source
0041	A	English (Latin)
042F	Я	Russian (Cyrillic)
OE09	ฦ	Thai
13EA	Ꮪ	Cherokee
211E	℞	Letterlike Symbols
21CC	⇌	Arrows
282F	⠯	Braille
345F	低	Chinese/Japanese/Korean (Common)

Figure 3.6 A few characters in the Unicode character set   3-35

Text Compression

- It is important that we find ways to store and transmit text efficiently, which means we must find ways to compress text.
  - keyword encoding
  - run-length encoding
  - Huffman encoding

3-36

Notes

Keyword Encoding

- Frequently used words are replaced with a single character. For example,

Word	Symbol
as	^
the	~
and	+
that	$
must	&
well	%
those	#

3-37

Keyword Encoding

- Given the following paragraph,

  The human body is composed of many independent systems, such as the circulatory system, the respiratory system, and the reproductive system. Not only must all systems work independently, they must interact and cooperate as well. Overall health is a function of the well-being of separate systems, as well as how these separate systems work in concert.

3-38

Keyword Encoding

- The encoded paragraph is

  The human body is composed of many independent systems, such ^ ~ circulatory system, ~ respiratory system, + ~ reproductive system. Not only & each system work independently, they & interact + cooperate ^ %. Overall health is a function of ~ %- being of separate systems, ^ % ^ how # separate systems work in concert.

3-39

Notes

Keyword Encoding

- There are a total of 349 characters in the original paragraph including spaces and punctuation. The encoded paragraph contains 314 characters, resulting in a savings of 35 characters. The compression ratio for this example is 314/349 or approximately 0.9.
- The characters we use to encode cannot be part of the original text.

3-40

Run-Length Encoding

- A single character may be repeated over and over again in a long sequence. This type of repetition doesn't generally take place in English text, but often occurs in large data streams.
- In run-length encoding, a sequence of repeated characters is replaced by a *flag character*, followed by the repeated character, followed by a single digit that indicates how many times the character is repeated.

3-41

Run-Length Encoding

- AAAAAAA would be encoded as *A7
- *n5*x9ccc*h6 some other text *k8eee would be decoded into the following original text nnnnnxxxxxxxxxcccchhhhhh some other text kkkkkkkkeee
- The original text contains 51 characters, and the encoded string contains 35 characters, giving us a compression ratio in this example of 35/51 or approximately 0.68.
- Since we are using one character for the repetition count, it seems that we can't encode repetition lengths greater than nine. Instead of interpreting the count character as an ASCII digit, we could interpret it as a binary number.

3-42

Notes

Huffman Encoding

- Why should the character "X", which is seldom used in text, take up the same number of bits as the blank, which is used very frequently? Huffman codes using variable-length bit strings to represent each character.
- A few characters may be represented by five bits, and another few by six bits, and yet another few by seven bits, and so forth.

3-43

Huffman Encoding

- If we use only a few bits to represent characters that appear often and reserve longer bit strings for characters that don't appear often, the overall size of the document being represented is smaller.

3-44

Huffman Encoding

- For example

Huffman Code	Character
00	A
01	E
100	L
110	O
111	R
1010	B
1011	D

3-45

Notes

Huffman Encoding

- DOORBELL would be encode in binary as
  101111011011101001100100.
- If we used a fixed-size bit string to represent
  each character (say, 8 bits), then the binary from
  of the original string would be 64 bits. The
  Huffman encoding for that string is 25 bits long,
  giving a compression ratio of 25/64, or
  approximately 0.39.
- An important characteristic of any Huffman
  encoding is that no bit string used to represent a
  character is the prefix of any other bit string used
  to represent a character.

3-46

Representing Audio Information

- We perceive sound when a series of air
  compressions vibrate a membrane in our
  ear, which sends signals to our brain.
- A stereo sends an electrical signal to a
  speaker to produce sound. This signal is
  an analog representation of the sound
  wave. The voltage in the signal varies in
  direct proportion to the sound wave.

3-47

Representing Audio Information

- To digitize the signal we periodically
  measure the voltage of the signal and
  record the appropriate numeric value. The
  process is called *sampling*.
- In general, a sampling rate of around
  40,000 times per second is enough to
  create a reasonable sound reproduction.

3-48

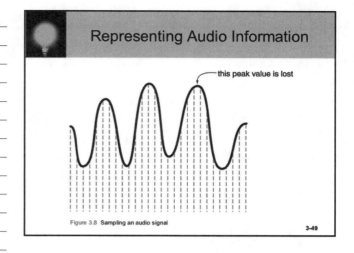

Representing Audio Information

this peak value is lost

Figure 3.8 Sampling an audio signal

3-49

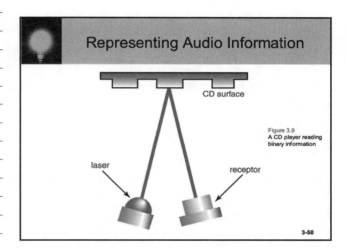

Representing Audio Information

CD surface

Figure 3.9
A CD player reading
binary information

laser

receptor

3-50

Representing Audio Information

- A compact disk (CD) stores audio information digitally. On the surface of the CD are microscopic pits that represent binary digits. A low intensity laser is pointed as the disc. The laser light reflects strongly if the surface is smooth and reflects poorly if the surface is pitted.

3-51

Notes

Audio Formats

- Audio Formats
  - WAV, AU, AIFF, VQF, and MP3.
- MP3 is dominant
  - MP3 is short for MPEG-2, audio layer 3 file.
  - MP3 employs both lossy and lossless compression. First it analyzes the frequency spread and compares it to mathematical models of human psychoacoustics (the study of the interrelation between the ear and the brain), then it discards information that can't be heard by humans. Then the bit stream is compressed using a form of Huffman encoding to achieve additional compression.

3-52

Representing Images and Graphics

- Color is our perception of the various frequencies of light that reach the retinas of our eyes.
- Our retinas have three types of color photoreceptor cone cells that respond to different sets of frequencies. These photoreceptor categories correspond to the colors of red, green, and blue.

3-53

Representing Images and Graphics

- Color is often expressed in a computer as an RGB (red-green-blue) value, which is actually three numbers that indicate the relative contribution of each of these three primary colors.
- For example, an RGB value of (255, 255, 0) maximizes the contribution of red and green, and minimizes the contribution of blue, which results in a bright yellow.

3-54

Notes

_____

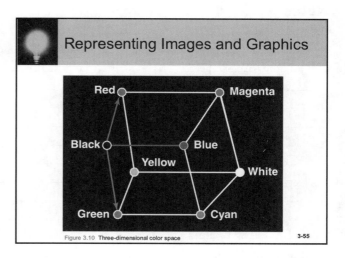

Representing Images and Graphics

Figure 3.10 Three-dimensional color space

3-55

Representing Images and Graphics

- The amount of data that is used to represent a color is called the _color depth_.
- _HiColor_ is a term that indicates a 16-bit color depth. Five bits are used for each number in an RGB value and the extra bit is sometimes used to represent transparency. _TrueColor_ indicates a 24-bit color depth. Therefore, each number in an RGB value gets eight bits.

3-56

Representing Images and Graphics

RGB Value			Actual Color
Red	**Green**	**Blue**	
0	0	0	black
255	255	255	white
255	255	0	yellow
255	130	255	pink
146	81	0	brown
157	95	82	purple
140	0	0	maroon

3-57

Notes

Indexed Color

- A particular application such as a browser may support only a certain number of specific colors, creating a palette from which to choose. For example, the Netscape Navigator's color palette is

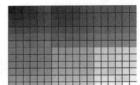

Figure 3.11
The Netscape color palette

3-58

Digitized Images and Graphics

- Digitizing a picture is the act of representing it as a collection of individual dots called **pixels**.
- The number of pixels used to represent a picture is called the **resolution**.
- The storage of image information on a pixel-by-pixel basis is called a **raster-graphics format**. Several popular raster file formats including bitmap (BMP), GIF, and JPEG.

3-59

Digitized Images and Graphics

Figure 3.12 A digitized picture composed of many individual pixels

3-60

Notes

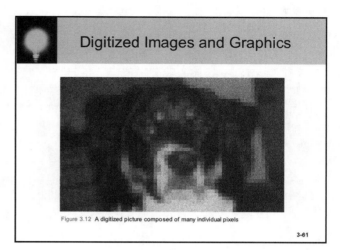

Digitized Images and Graphics

Figure 3.12 A digitized picture composed of many individual pixels

3-61

Vector Graphics

- Instead of assigning colors to pixels as we do in raster graphics, a vector-graphics format describe an image in terms of lines and geometric shapes. A vector graphic is a series of commands that describe a line's direction, thickness, and color. The file size for these formats tend to be small because every pixel does not have to be accounted for.

3-62

Vector Graphics

- Vector graphics can be resized mathematically, and these changes can be calculated dynamically as needed.
- However, vector graphics is not good for representing real-world images.

3-63

Representing Video

- A video codec COmpressor/DECompressor refers to the methods used to shrink the size of a movie to allow it to be played on a computer or over a network. Almost all video codecs use lossy compression to minimize the huge amounts of data associated with video.

3-64

Representing Video

- Two types of compression, **temporal** and **spatial**.

  Temporal compression A technique based differences between consecutive frames. If most of an image in two frames hasn't changed, why should we waste space to duplicate all of the similar information?

  Spatial compression A technique based on removing redundant information within a frame. This problem is essentially the same as that faced when compressing still images.

3-65

Chapter 4: Gates and Circuits

Notes

Computer Science Illuminated
SECOND EDITION
Nell Dale • John Lewis

Chapter 4
Gates and Circuits

Chapter Goals

- Identify the basic gates and describe the behavior of each
- Describe how gates are implemented using transistors
- Combine basic gates into circuits
- Describe the behavior of a gate or circuit using Boolean expressions, truth tables, and logic diagrams

4–2

Chapter Goals

- Compare and contrast a half adder and a full adder
- Describe how a multiplexer works
- Explain how an S-R latch operates
- Describe the characteristics of the four generations of integrated circuits

4–3

Computers and Electricity

- **Gate** A device that performs a basic operation on electrical signals

- **Circuits** Gates combined to perform more complicated tasks

4–4

Computers and Electricity

- There are three different, but equally powerful, notational methods for describing the behavior of gates and circuits
  - Boolean expressions
  - logic diagrams
  - truth tables

4–5

Computers and Electricity

- **Boolean expressions** Expressions in Boolean algebra, a mathematical notation for expressing two-valued logic

This algebraic notation are an elegant and powerful way to demonstrate the activity of electrical circuits

4–6

Computers and Electricity

- **Logic diagram** A graphical representation of a circuit
    Each type of gate is represented by a specific graphical symbol
- **Truth table** A table showing all possible input value and the associated output values

4–7

Gates

- Let's examine the processing of the following six types of gates
    - NOT
    - AND
    - OR
    - XOR
    - NAND
    - NOR
- Typically, logic diagrams are black and white, and the gates are distinguished only by their shape

4–8

NOT Gate

- A NOT gate accepts one input value and produces one output value

Boolean Expression	Logic Diagram Symbol	Truth Table	
X = A'	A ▷o X	A	X
		0	1
		1	0

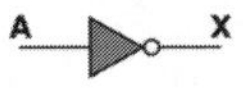

Figure 4.1 Various representations of a NOT gate

4–9

NOT Gate

- By definition, if the input value for a NOT gate is 0, the output value is 1, and if the input value is 1, the output is 0

- A NOT gate is sometimes referred to as an *inverter* because it inverts the input value

4–10

AND Gate

- An AND gate accepts two input signals

- If the two input values for an AND gate are both 1, the output is 1; otherwise, the output is 0

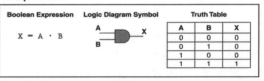

Boolean Expression	Logic Diagram Symbol	Truth Table		
		A	B	X
X = A · B		0	0	0
		0	1	0
		1	0	0
		1	1	1

Figure 4.2 **Various representations of an AND gate**

4–11

OR Gate

- If the two input values are both 0, the output value is 0; otherwise, the output is 1

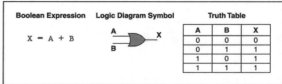

Boolean Expression	Logic Diagram Symbol	Truth Table		
		A	B	X
X = A + B		0	0	0
		0	1	1
		1	0	1
		1	1	1

Figure 4.3 **Various representations of a OR gate**

4–12

Notes

XOR Gate

- XOR, or *exclusive* OR, gate
  - An XOR gate produces 0 if its two inputs are the same, and a 1 otherwise
  - Note the difference between the XOR gate and the OR gate; they differ only in one input situation
  - When both input signals are 1, the OR gate produces a 1 and the XOR produces a 0

4–13

XOR Gate

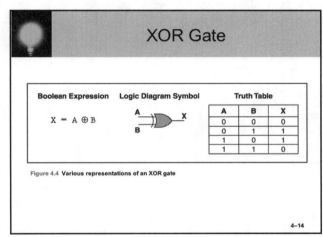

Figure 4.4 **Various representations of an XOR gate**

4–14

NAND and NOR Gates

- The NAND and NOR gates are essentially the opposite of the AND and OR gates, respectively

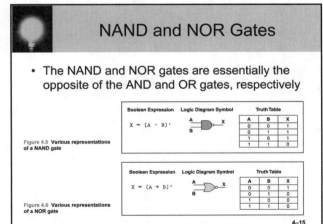

4–15

Notes

Review of Gate Processing

- A NOT gate inverts its single input value

- An AND gate produces 1 if both input values are 1

- An OR gate produces 1 if one or the other or both input values are 1

4–16

Review of Gate Processing

- An XOR gate produces 1 if one or the other (but not both) input values are 1

- A NAND gate produces the opposite results of an AND gate

- A NOR gate produces the opposite results of an OR gate

4–17

Gates with More Inputs

- Gates can be designed to accept three or more input values

- A three-input AND gate, for example, produces an output of 1 only if all input values are 1

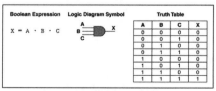

Figure 4.7 Various representations of a three-input AND gate

4–18

Constructing Gates

- **Transistor** A device that acts, depending on the voltage level of an input signal, either as a wire that conducts electricity or as a resistor that blocks the flow of electricity
    - A transistor has no moving parts, yet acts like a switch
    - It is made of a **semiconductor** material, which is neither a particularly good conductor of electricity, such as copper, nor a particularly good insulator, such as rubber

4–19

Constructing Gates

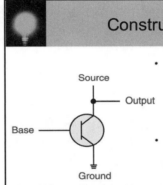

- A transistor has three terminals
    - A source
    - A base
    - An emitter, typically connected to a ground wire
- If the electrical signal is grounded, it is allowed to flow through an alternative route to the ground (literally) where it can do no harm

Figure 4.8 **The connections of a transistor**

4–20

Constructing Gates

- It turns out that, because the way a transistor works, the easiest gates to create are the NOT, NAND, and NOR gates

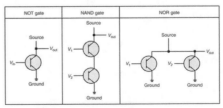

Figure 4.9 **Constructing gates using transistors**

4–21

Notes

Circuits

- Two general categories
  - In a **combinational circuit**, the input values explicitly determine the output
  - In a **sequential circuit**, the output is a function of the input values as well as the existing state of the circuit

- As with gates, we can describe the operations of entire circuits using three notations
  - Boolean expressions
  - logic diagrams
  - truth tables

4–22

Combinational Circuits

- Gates are combined into circuits by using the output of one gate as the input for another

Page 99

4–23

Combinational Circuits

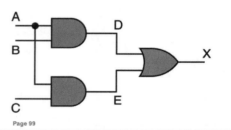

A	B	C	D	E	X
0	0	0	0	0	0
0	0	1	0	0	0
0	1	0	0	0	0
0	1	1	0	0	0
1	0	0	0	0	0
1	0	1	0	1	1
1	1	0	1	0	1
1	1	1	1	1	1

Page 100

- Because there are three inputs to this circuit, eight rows are required to describe all possible input combinations

- This same circuit using Boolean algebra is (AB + AC)

4–24

46

y

Chapter 4

Notes

Now let's go the other way; let's take a Boolean expression and draw

- Consider the following Boolean expression $A(B + C)$

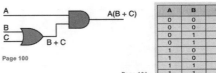

Page 100

Page 101

A	B	C	B + C	A(B+C)
0	0	0	0	0
0	0	1	1	0
0	1	0	1	0
0	1	1	1	0
1	0	0	0	0
1	0	1	1	1
1	1	0	1	1
1	1	1	1	1

- Now compare the final result column in this truth table to the truth table for the previous example
  - They are identical

4–25

Now let's go the other way; let's take a Boolean expression and draw

- We have therefore just demonstrated **circuit equivalence**
  - That is, both circuits produce the exact same output for each input value combination
- Boolean algebra allows us to apply provable mathematical principles to help us design logical circuits

4–26

Properties of Boolean Algebra

Property	AND	OR
Commutative	$AB = BA$	$A + B = B + A$
Associative	$(AB)C = A(BC)$	$(A + B) + C = A + (B + C)$
Distributive	$A(B + C) = (AB) + (AC)$	$A + (BC) = (A + B)(A + C)$
Identity	$A1 = A$	$A + 0 = A$
Complement	$A(A') = 0$	$A + (A') = 1$
DeMorgan's law	$(AB)' = A' OR B'$	$(A + B)' = A'B'$

Page 101

4–27

Adders

- At the digital logic level, addition is performed in binary

- Addition operations are carried out by special circuits called, appropriately, **adders**

4–28

Adders

- The result of adding two binary digits could produce a *carry value*

- Recall that 1 + 1 = 10 in base two

- A circuit that computes the sum of two bits and produces the correct carry bit is called a **half adder**

A	B	Sum	Carry
0	0	0	0
0	1	1	0
1	0	1	0
1	1	0	1

Page 103

4–29

Adders

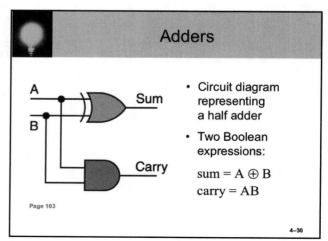

- Circuit diagram representing a half adder

- Two Boolean expressions:

$$sum = A \oplus B$$
$$carry = AB$$

Page 103

4–30

Notes

_____

_____

_____

_____

_____

_____

_____

_____

_____

_____

_____

_____

_____

_____

_____

_____

_____

_____

_____

_____

_____

_____

_____

_____

_____

_____

_____

_____

_____

_____

_____

_____

_____

_____

_____

_____

_____

_____

_____

_____

_____

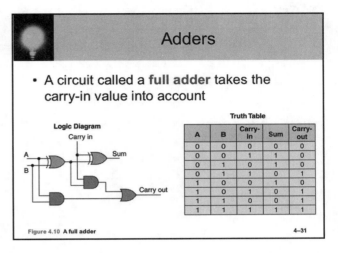

Adders

- A circuit called a **full adder** takes the carry-in value into account

Truth Table

A	B	Carry-in	Sum	Carry-out
0	0	0	0	0
0	0	1	1	0
0	1	0	1	0
0	1	1	0	1
1	0	0	1	0
1	0	1	0	1
1	1	0	0	1
1	1	1	1	1

Logic Diagram

Figure 4.10 **A full adder**

4–31

Multiplexers

- **Multiplexer** is a general circuit that produces a single output signal
  - The output is equal to one of several input signals to the circuit
  - The multiplexer selects which input signal is used as an output signal based on the value represented by a few more input signals, called _select signals_ or _select control lines_

4–32

Multiplexers

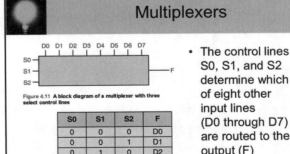

Figure 4.11 **A block diagram of a multiplexer with three select control lines**

S0	S1	S2	F
0	0	0	D0
0	0	1	D1
0	1	0	D2
0	1	1	D3
1	0	0	D4
1	0	1	D5
1	1	0	D6
1	1	1	D7

- The control lines S0, S1, and S2 determine which of eight other input lines (D0 through D7) are routed to the output (F)

Page 105

4–33

Circuits as Memory

- Digital circuits can be used to store information

- These circuits form a sequential circuit, because the output of the circuit is also used as input to the circuit

4–34

Circuits as Memory

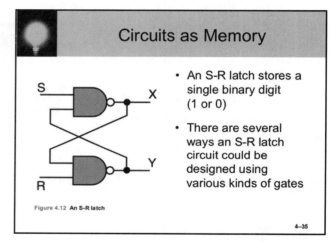

- An S-R latch stores a single binary digit (1 or 0)

- There are several ways an S-R latch circuit could be designed using various kinds of gates

Figure 4.12 **An S-R latch**

4–35

Circuits as Memory

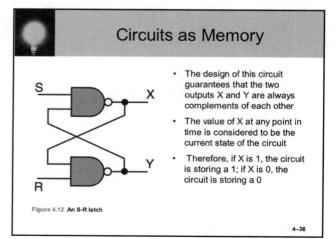

- The design of this circuit guarantees that the two outputs X and Y are always complements of each other

- The value of X at any point in time is considered to be the current state of the circuit

- Therefore, if X is 1, the circuit is storing a 1; if X is 0, the circuit is storing a 0

Figure 4.12 **An S-R latch**

4–36

Notes

Integrated Circuits

- **Integrated circuit** (also called a *chip*) A piece of silicon on which multiple gates have been embedded

  These silicon pieces are mounted on a plastic or ceramic package with pins along the edges that can be soldered onto circuit boards or inserted into appropriate sockets

4–37

Integrated Circuits

- Integrated circuits (IC) are classified by the number of gates contained in them

Abbreviation	Name	Number of Gates
SSI	Small-Scale Integration	1 to 10
MSI	Medium-Scale Integration	10 to 100
LSI	Large-Scale Integration	100 to 100,000
VLSI	Very-Large-Scale Integration	more than 100,000

Page 107

4–38

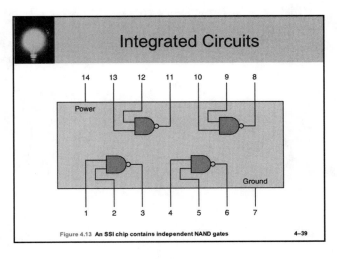

Figure 4.13 **An SSI chip contains independent NAND gates**

4–39

CPU Chips

- The most important integrated circuit in any computer is the Central Processing Unit, or CPU

- Each CPU chip has a large number of pins through which essentially all communication in a computer system occurs

4–40

Chapter 5: Computing Components

Notes

Computer Science Illuminated

SECOND EDITION

Nell Dale • John Lewis

Chapter 5

Computing Components

Chapter Goals

- Read an ad for a computer and understand the jargon

- List the components and their function in a von Neumann machine

- Describe the fetch-decode-execute cycle of the von Neumann machine

5-2

Chapter Goals

- Describe how computer memory is organized and accessed

- Name and describe different auxiliary storage devices

- Define three alternative parallel computer configurations

5-3

Notes

Computer Components

- Consider the following ad

Dell Dimension 4600 Series
Exceptional Performance, Small Design

- Intel® Pentium® 4 Processor at 3.06GHz
- 512MB Dual Channel shared SDRAM at 333MHz
- 80GB Ultra ATA/100 Hard Drive
- 17" Flat-Panel Display
- Integrated Intel® Extreme Graphics 2
- 2X DVD+R/+RW Drive with CD-RW
- Integrated 5.1 Audio with Dolby Digital 5.1 capability
- Roxio Easy CD Creator®
- Altec Lansing® ADA745 4.1 Surround Sound Speakers with Subwoofer
- 56K PCI Data/Fax Modem
- WordPerfect® Productivity Pack with Quicken New User Edition
- 6 months of America Online Membership included

5-4

Sizes in Perspective

- Admiral Grace Murray Hopper
  - A coil of wire nearly 1,000 feet long
    - Distance traveled by an electron along the wire in the space of a microsecond
  - A short piece of wire
    - In the space of a nanosecond
  - A bag containing grains of pepper
    - In the space of a picosecond

5-5

Sizes in Perspective

Power of 10	Power of 2	Value of Power of 2	Prefix	Abbreviation	Derivation
10^{-12}			pico	p	Spanish for little
10^{-9}			nano	n	Greek for dwarf
10^{-6}			micro	μ	Greek for small
10^{-3}			milli	m	Latin for thousand
10^{3}	2^{10}	1024	kilo	K	Greek for thousandth
10^{6}	2^{20}	1,048,576	mega	M	Greek for large
10^{9}	2^{30}	1,073,741,824	giga	G	Greek for giant
10^{12}	2^{40}	not enough room	tera	T	Greek for monster
10^{15}	2^{50}	not enough room	peta	P	Greek prefix for five

5-6

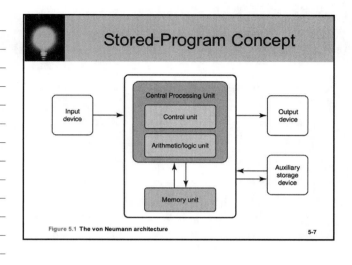

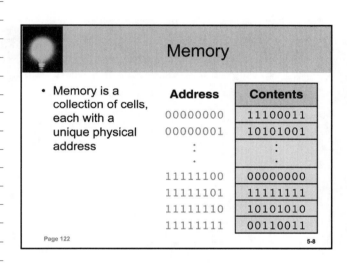

Arithmetic/Logic Unit

- Performing basic arithmetic operations such as adding

- Performing logical operations such as AND, OR, and NOT

- Most modern ALUs have a small amount of special storage units called **registers**

5-9

Input/Output Units

- **Input Unit** A device through which data and programs from the outside world are entered into the computer
  - Keyboard, the mouse, and scanning devices

- **Output unit** A device through which results stored in the computer memory are made available to the outside world
  - Printers and video display terminals

5-10

Control Unit

- **Control unit** The organizing force in the computer

- There are two registers in the control unit
  - The **instruction register** (IR) contains the instruction that is being executed
  - The **program counter** (PC) contains the address of the next instruction to be executed

- ALU and the control unit called the **Central Processing Unit**, or CPU

5-11

Flow of Information

- The parts are connected to one another by a collection of wires called a bus

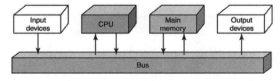

Figure 5.2 Data flow through a von Neumann architecture

5-12

Notes

The Fetch-Execute Cycle

- Fetch the next instruction
- Decode the instruction
- Get data if needed
- Execute the instruction

5-13

Figure 5.3 The Fetch-Execute Cycle

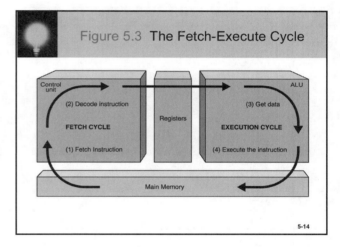

5-14

RAM and ROM

- RAM stands for **Random Access Memory**
  - Inherent in the idea of being able to access each location is the ability to change the contents of each location
- ROM stands for **Read Only Memory**
  - The contents in locations in ROM cannot be changed
- RAM is volatile, ROM is not
  - This means that RAM does not retain its bit configuration when the power is turned off, but ROM does

5-15

Notes

Secondary Storage Devices

- Because most of main memory is volatile and limited, it is essential that there be other types of storage devices where programs and data can be stored when they are no longer being processed

- Secondary storage devices can be installed within the computer box at the factory or added later as needed

5-16

Magnetic Tape

- The first truly mass auxiliary storage device was the magnetic tape drive

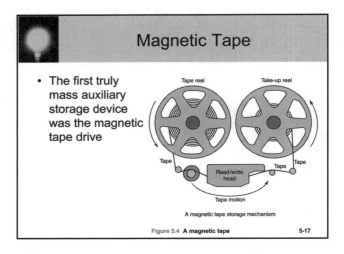

A magnetic tape storage mechanism

Figure 5.4 **A magnetic tape**   5-17

Magnetic Disks

- A read/write head travels across a spinning magnetic disk, retrieving or recording data

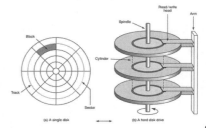

Figure 5.5
The organization of a magnetic disk

5-18

Notes

Compact Disks

- A CD drive uses a laser to read information stored optically on a plastic disk
- CD-ROM is Read-Only Memory
- DVD stands for Digital Versatile Disk

5-19

Touch Screens

- **Touch screen** A computer monitor that can respond to the user touching the screen with a stylus or finger
- There are three types
    - Resistive
    - Capacitive
    - Infrared
    - Surface acoustic wave (SAW)

5-20

Touch Screens

- Resistive touch screen A screen made up of two layers of electrically conductive material.
    - One layer has vertical lines, the other has horizontal lines.
    - When the top layer is pressed, it comes in contact with the second layer which allows electrical current to flow.
    - The specific vertical and horizontal lines that make contact dictate the location on the screen that was touched.

5-21

Notes

Touch Screens

- **Capacitive touch screen** A screen made up of a laminate applied over a glass screen.
  - The laminate conducts electricity in all directions, and a very small current is applied equally on the four corners.
  - When the screen is touched, current flows to the finger or stylus.
  - The location of the touch on the screen is determined by comparing how strong the flow of electricity is from each corner.

5-22

Touch Screens

- **Infrared touch screen** A screen with crisscrossing horizontal and vertical beams of infrared light
  - Sensors on opposite sides of the screen detect the beams.
  - When the user breaks the beams by touching the screen, the location of the break can be determined.

5-23

Touch Screens

- **Surface acoustic wave (SAW)** A screen with crisscrossing high frequency sound waves across the horizontal and vertical axes.
  - When a finger touches the surface, the corresponding sensors detect the interruption and determine the location of the touch.

5-24

Notes

Synchronous processing

- One approach to parallelism is to have multiple processors apply the same program to multiple data sets

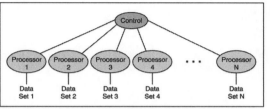

Figure 5.7 **Processors in a synchronous computing environment**

5-25

Pipelining

- Arranges processors in tandem, where each processor contributes one part to an overall computation

Figure 5.8 **Processors in a pipeline**

5-26

Independent Processing with Shared Memory

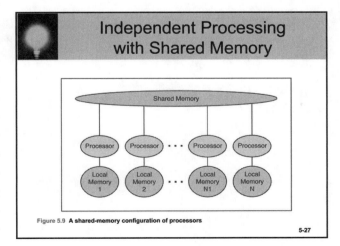

Figure 5.9 **A shared-memory configuration of processors**

5-27

Notes

Computer Science Illuminated
SECOND EDITION
Nell Dale • John Lewis

Chapter 6

Problem Solving
and Algorithm Design

Chapter Goals

- Determine whether a problem is suitable for a computer solution

- Describe the computer problem-solving process and relate it to Polya's How to Solve It list

- Distinguish between following an algorithm and developing one

- Apply top-down design methodology to develop an algorithm to solve a problem

6-2

Chapter Goals

- Define the key terms in object-oriented design

- Apply object-oriented design methodology to develop a collection of interacting objects to solve a problem

- Discuss the following threads as they relate to problem solving: information hiding, abstraction, naming things, and testing

6-3

Notes

_____
_____
_____
_____
_____
_____
_____
_____
_____
_____
_____
_____
_____
_____
_____
_____
_____
_____
_____
_____
_____
_____
_____
_____
_____
_____
_____
_____
_____
_____
_____
_____
_____
_____
_____

Problem Solving

- **Problem solving** The act of finding a solution to a perplexing, distressing, vexing, or unsettled question

6-4

Problem Solving

- G. Polya wrote _How to Solve It: A New Aspect of Mathematical Method_
- His How to Solve It list is quite general
  - Written in the context of solving mathematical problems
  - The list becomes applicable to all types of problems

6-5

Ask Questions...

- ...to understand the problem
  - _What do I know about the problem?_
  - _What is the information that I have to process in order the find the solution?_
  - _What does the solution look like?_
  - _What sort of special cases exist?_
  - _How will I recognize that I have found the solution?_

6-6

Notes

Look for Familiar Things

- You should never reinvent the wheel

- In computing, you see certain problems again and again in different guises

- A good programmer sees a task, or perhaps part of a task (a subtask), that has been solved before and plugs in the solution

6-7

Divide and Conquer

- Break up a large problem into smaller units that we can handle
  - Applies the concept of abstraction
  - The divide-and-conquer approach can be applied over and over again until each subtask is manageable

6-8

Algorithms

- **Algorithm** A set of instructions for solving a problem or subproblem in a finite amount of time using a finite amount of data

- The instructions must be unambiguous

6-9

Notes

_____
_____
_____
_____
_____
_____
_____
_____
_____
_____
_____
_____
_____
_____
_____
_____
_____
_____
_____
_____
_____
_____
_____
_____
_____
_____
_____
_____
_____
_____
_____
_____
_____
_____
_____
_____
_____

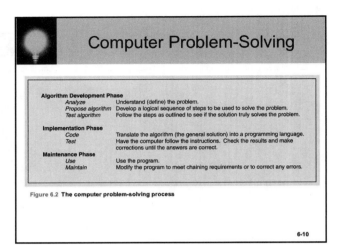

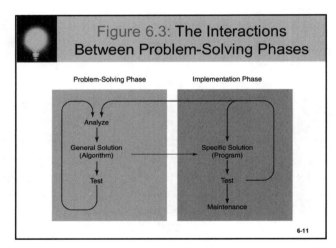

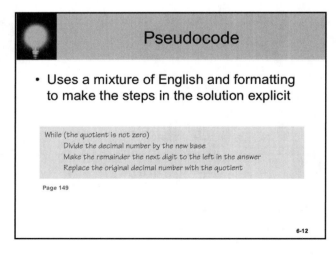

Notes

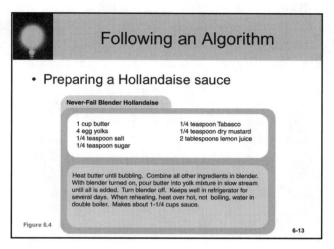

Following an Algorithm

- Preparing a Hollandaise sauce

Never-Fail Blender Hollandaise

1 cup butter	1/4 teaspoon Tabasco
4 egg yolks	1/4 teaspoon dry mustard
1/4 teaspoon salt	2 tablespoons lemon juice
1/4 teaspoon sugar	

Heat butter until bubbling. Combine all other ingredients in blender. With blender turned on, pour butter into yolk mixture in slow stream until all is added. Turn blender off. Keeps well in refrigerator for several days. When reheating, heat over hot, not boiling, water in double boiler. Makes about 1-1/4 cups sauce.

Figure 6.4

6-13

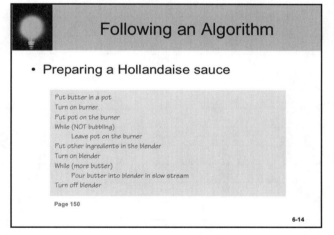

Following an Algorithm

- Preparing a Hollandaise sauce

```
Put butter in a pot
Turn on burner
Put pot on the burner
While (NOT bubbling)
        Leave pot on the burner
Put other ingredients in the blender
Turn on blender
While (more butter)
        Pour butter into blender in slow stream
Turn off blender
```

Page 150

6-14

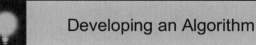

Developing an Algorithm

- The plan must be suitable in a suitable form

- Two methodologies that currently used
  - Top-down design
  - Object-oriented design

6-15

Top-Down Design

- Breaking the problem into a set of subproblems called **modules**

- Creating a hierarchical structure of problems and subproblems (modules)

6-16

Top-Down Design

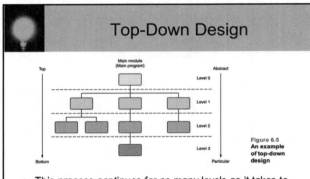

Figure 6.5
An example of top-down design

- This process continues for as many levels as it takes to expand every task to the smallest details

- A step that needs to be expanded is an abstract step

6-17

A General Example

- Planning a large party

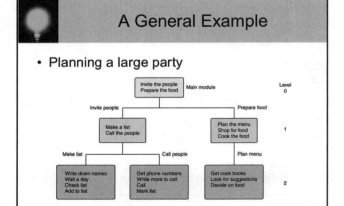

Figure 6.6 **Subdividing the party planning**

6-18

Notes

A Computer Example

- Problem
  - Create an address list that includes each person's name, address, telephone number, and e-mail address
  - This list should then be printed in alphabetical order
  - The names to be included in the list are on scraps of paper and business cards

6-19

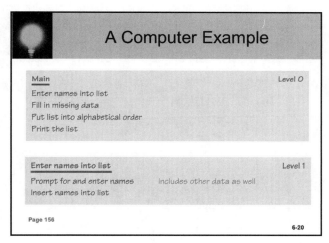

A Computer Example

Main	Level 0
Enter names into list	
Fill in missing data	
Put list into alphabetical order	
Print the list	

Enter names into list	Level 1
Prompt for and enter names	includes other data as well
Insert names into list	

Page 156

6-20

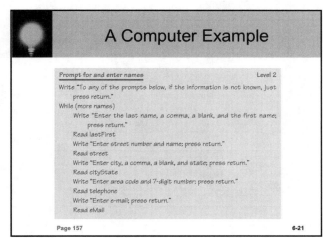

A Computer Example

Prompt for and enter names	Level 2

Write "To any of the prompts below, if the information is not known, just press return."
While (more names)
    Write "Enter the last name, a comma, a blank, and the first name; press return."
    Read lastFirst
    Write "Enter street number and name; press return."
    Read street
    Write "Enter city, a comma, a blank, and state; press return."
    Read cityState
    Write "Enter area code and 7-digit number; press return."
    Read telephone
    Write "Enter e-mail; press return."
    Read eMail

Page 157

6-21

Notes

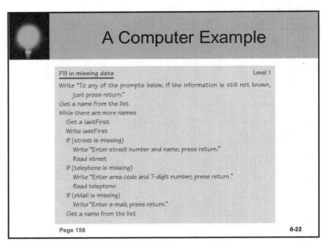

A Computer Example

Fill in missing data   Level 1

Write "To any of the prompts below, if the information is still not known,
   just press return."
Get a name from the list
While there are more names
   Get a lastFirst
   Write lastFirst
   If (street is missing)
      Write "Enter street number and name; press return."
      Read street
   If (telephone is missing)
      Write "Enter area code and 7-digit number; press return."
      Read telephone
   If (eMail is missing)
      Write "Enter e-mail; press return."
   Get a name from the list

Page 158   6-22

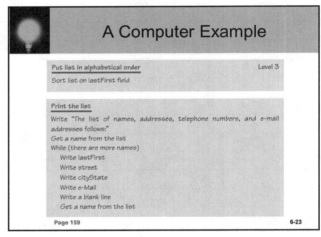

A Computer Example

Put list in alphabetical order   Level 3

Sort list on lastFirst field

Print the list

Write "The list of names, addresses, telephone numbers, and e-mail
addresses follows:"
Get a name from the list
While (there are more names)
   Write lastFirst
   Write street
   Write cityState
   Write e-Mail
   Write a blank line
   Get a name from the list

Page 159   6-23

Testing the Algorithm

- The process itself must be tested

- Testing at the algorithm development
  phase involves looking at each level of the
  top-down design

6-24

Notes

_____
_____
_____
_____
_____
_____
_____
_____
_____
_____
_____
_____
_____
_____
_____
_____
_____
_____
_____
_____
_____
_____
_____
_____
_____
_____
_____
_____
_____
_____
_____
_____
_____
_____
_____
_____
_____

Testing the Algorithm

- **Desk checking** Working through a design at a desk with a pencil and paper
- **Walk-through** Manual simulation of the design by the team members, taking sample data values and simulating the design using the sample data
- **Inspection** One person (not the designer) reads the design (handed out in advance) line by line while the others point out errors

6-25

Object-Oriented Design

- A problem-solving methodology that produces a solution to a problem in terms of self-contained entities called *objects*
- **Object** A thing or entity that makes sense within the context of the problem
  For example, a student

6-26

Object-Oriented Design

- A group of similar objects is described by an **object class**, or **class**
- A class contains fields that represent the properties and behaviors of the class
  - A **field** can contain data value(s) and/or methods (subprograms)
  - A **method** is a named algorithm that manipulates the data values in the object

6-27

Notes

Relationships Between Classes

- Containment
  - "part-of"
  - An address class may be part of the definition of a student class

- Inheritance
  - Classes can inherit data and behavior from other classes
  - "is-a"

6-28

Object-Oriented Design Methodology

- Four stages to the decomposition process
  - Brainstorming
  - Filtering
  - Scenarios
  - Responsibility algorithms

6-29

CRC Cards

Class Name:	Superclass:		Subclasses:
Responsibilities		Collaborations	

Page 165

6-30

Notes

Brainstorming

- A group problem-solving technique that involves the spontaneous contribution of ideas from all members of the group
  - All ideas are potential good ideas
  - Think fast and furiously first, and ponder later
  - A little humor can be a powerful force
- Brainstorming is designed to produce a list of candidate classes

6-31

Filtering

- Determine which are the core classes in the problem solution
- There may be two classes in the list that have many common attributes and behaviors
- There may be classes that really don't belong in the problem solution

6-32

Scenarios

- Assign responsibilities to each class
- There are two types of responsibilities
  - What a class must know about itself (knowledge responsibilities)
  - What a class must be able to do (behavior responsibilities)

6-33

Scenarios

- Each class **encapsulates** its data but shares their values through knowledge responsibilities.

- **Encapsulation** is the bundling of data and actions in such a way that the logical properties of the data and actions are separated from the implementation details

6-34

Responsibility Algorithms

- The algorithms must be written for the responsibilities
    - Knowledge responsibilities usually just return the contents of one of an object's variables
    - Action responsibilities are a little more complicated, often involving calculations

6-35

Computer Example

- Let's repeat the problem-solving process for creating an address list

- Brainstorming and filtering
    - Circling the nouns and underlining the verbs

Create an address list that includes each person's name, address, telephone number, and e-mail address. This list should then be printed in alphabetical order. The names to be included in the list are on scraps of paper and business cards.

Page 171   6-36

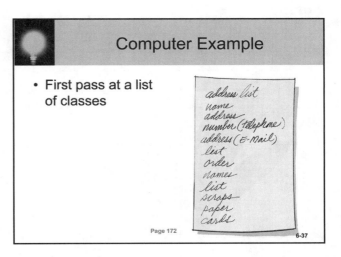

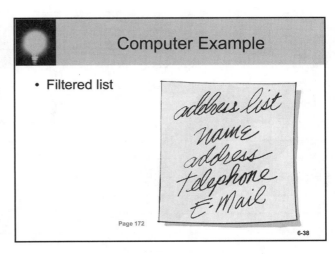

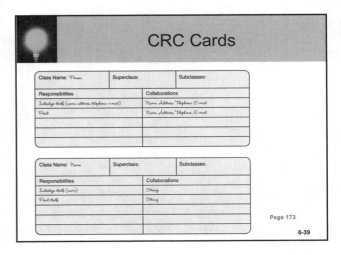

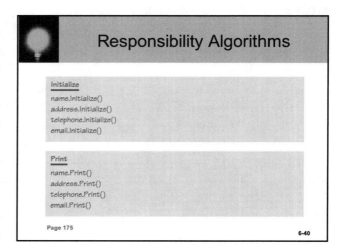

Responsibility Algorithms

Initialize
name.Initialize()
address.Initialize()
telephone.Initialize()
email.Initialize()

Print
name.Print()
address.Print()
telephone.Print()
email.Print()

Page 175

6-40

Information Hiding/Abstraction

- **Information Hiding** and **Abstraction** are two sides of the same coin.
  - **Information Hiding** The practice of hiding the details of a module with the goal of controlling access to the details of the module.
  - **Abstraction** A model of a complex system that includes only the details essential to the viewer.

6-41

Information Hiding/Abstraction

- Abstraction is the result with the details hidden
  - **Data abstraction** Separation of the logical view of data from their implementation.
  - **Procedural abstraction** Separation of the logical view of actions from their implementation.
  - **Control abstraction** Separation of the logical view of a control structure from its implementation.

6-42

Programming Languages

- Instructions written in a **programming language** can be *translated* into the instructions that a computer can execute directly

- **Program** A meaningful sequence of instructions for a computer
  - **Syntax** The part that says how the instructions of the language can be put together
  - **Semantics** The part that says what the instructions mean

6-43

Notes

Chapter 7
Low-Level Programming Languages

Computer Science Illuminated
SECOND EDITION
Nell Dale • John Lewis

Chapter Goals

- List the operations that a computer can perform
- Discuss the relationship between levels of abstraction and the determination of concrete algorithm steps
- Describe the important features of the Pep/7 virtual machine
- Distinguish between immediate mode addressing and direct addressing

7-2

Chapter Goals

- Convert a simple algorithm into a machine-language program
- Distinguish between machine language and assembly language
- Describe the steps in creating and running an assembly-language program
- Convert a simple algorithm into an assembly-language program

7-3

Chapter Goals

- Distinguish between instructions to the assembler and instructions to be translated
- Describe two approaches to testing
- Design and implement a test plan for a simple assembly-language program

7-4

Computer Operations

- A computer is a programmable electronic device that can store, retrieve, and process data
- Data and instructions to manipulate the data are logically the same and can be stored in the same place
- Store, retrieve, and process are actions that the computer can perform on data

7-5

Machine Language

- **Machine language** The instructions built into the hardware of a particular computer
- Initially, humans had no choice but to write programs in machine language because other programming languages had not yet been invented

7-6

Machine Language

- Every processor type has its own set of specific machine instructions

- The relationship between the processor and the instructions it can carry out is completely integrated

- Each machine-language instruction does only one very low-level task

7-7

Pep/7: A Virtual Computer

- **Virtual computer** A hypothetical machine designed to contain the important features of real computers that we want to illustrate

- Pep/7
  - designed by Stanley Warford
  - has 32 machine-language instructions

- We are only going to examine a few of these instructions

7-8

Features in Pep/7

- The memory unit is made up of 4,096 bytes

- Pep/7 Registers/Status Bits Covered
  - The program counter (PC) (contains the address of the next instruction to be executed)
  - The instruction register (IR) (contains a copy of the instruction being executed)
  - The accumulator (A register)
  - Status bit N (1 if A register is negative; 0 otherwise)
  - Status bit Z (1 if the A register is 0; and 0 otherwise)

7-9

Notes

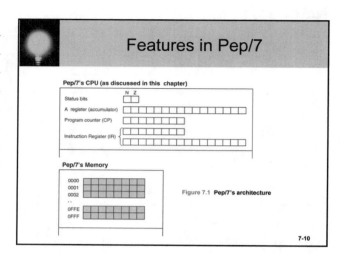

Features in Pep/7

Pep/7's CPU (as discussed in this chapter)

Status bits — N Z

A register (accumulator)

Program counter (CP)

Instruction Register (IR)

Pep/7's Memory

0000
0001
0002
..
0FFE
0FFF

Figure 7.1 **Pep/7's architecture**

7-10

Instruction Format

- There are two parts to an instruction
  - The 8-bit instruction specifier
  - And optionally, the 16-bit operand specifier

Instruction specifier

Operand specifier

(a) The two parts of an instruction

Addressing mode specifier
Register specifier
Operation code

Figure 7.2 **The Pep/7 instruction format**

(b) The instruction specifier part of an instruction

7-11

Instruction Format

- The instruction specifier is made up of several sections
  - The operation code
  - The register specifier
  - The addressing-mode specifier

7-12

Notes

Instruction Format

- The *operation code* specifies which instruction is to be carried out

- The 1-bit *register specifier* is 0 if register A (the accumulator) is involved, which is the case in this chapter.

- The 2-bit *addressing-mode specifier* says how to interpret the operand part of the instruction

7-13

Instruction Format

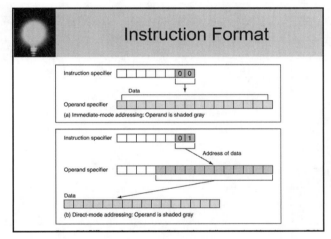

Some Sample Instructions

Opcode	Meaning of Instruction
00000	Stop execution
00001	Load operand into a register (either A of X)
00010	Store the contents of register (either A or X) into operand
00011	Add the operand to register (either A or X)
00100	Subtract the operand from register (either A or X)
11011	Character input to operand
11100	Character output from operand

Figure 7.3 **Subset of Pep/7 instructions**

7-15

A Program Example

- Let's write "Hello" on the screen

Module	Binary Instruction	Hex Instruction
Write "H"	11100000 0000000001001000	E0 0048
Write "e"	11100000 0000000001100101	E0 0065
Write "l"	11100000 0000000001101100	E0 006C
Write "l"	11100000 0000000001101100	E0 006C
Write "o"	11100000 0000000001101111	E0 006F
Stop	00000000	00

Page 200   7-16

Pep/7 Simulator

- A program that behaves just like the Pep/7 virtual machine behaves
- To run a program, we enter the hexadecimal code, byte by byte with blanks between each

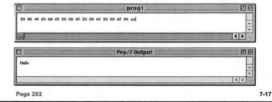

Page 202   7-17

Assembly Language

- **Assembly languages** A language that uses mnemonic codes to represent machine-language instructions
  - The programmer uses these alphanumeric codes in place of binary digits
  - A program called an assembler reads each of the instructions in mnemonic form and translates it into the machine-language equivalent

7-18

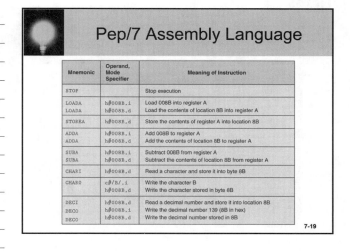

Pep/7 Assembly Language

Mnemonic	Operand, Mode Specifier	Meaning of Instruction
STOP		Stop execution
LOADA	h#008B,i	Load 008B into register A
LOADA	h#008B,d	Load the contents of location 8B into register A
STOREA	h#008B,d	Store the contents of register A into location 8B
ADDA	h#008B,i	Add 008B to register A
ADDA	h#008B,d	Add the contents of location 8B to register A
SUBA	h#008B,i	Subtract 008B from register A
SUBA	h#008B,d	Subtract the contents of location 8B from register A
CHARI	h#008B,d	Read a character and store it into byte 8B
CHARO	c#/B/,i	Write the character B
	h#008B,d	Write the character stored in byte 8B
DECI	h#008B,d	Read a decimal number and store it into location 8B
DECO	h#008B,i	Write the decimal number 139 (8B in hex)
DECO	h#008B,d	Write the decimal number stored in 8B

7-19

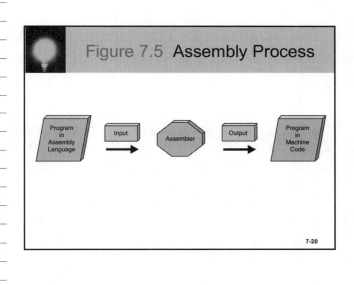

Figure 7.5 Assembly Process

7-20

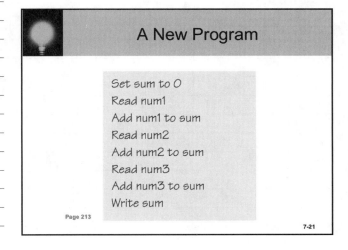

A New Program

Set sum to 0
Read num1
Add num1 to sum
Read num2
Add num2 to sum
Read num3
Add num3 to sum
Write sum

Page 213

7-21

Notes

Our Completed Program

```
          BR Main        ;branch to location Main
sum:    .WORD d#0       ;set up word with zero as the contents
num1:   .BLOCK d#2      ;set up a two byte block for num1
num2:   .BLOCK d#2      ;set up a two byte block for num2
num3:   .BLOCK d#2      ;set up a two byte block for num3
Main:   LOADA sum,d     ;load a copy of sum into accumulator
        DECI num1,d     ;read and store a decimal number in num1
        ADDA num1,d     ;add the contents of num1 to accumulator
        DECI num2,d     ;read and store a decimal number in num2
        ADDA num2,d     ;add the contents of num2 to accumulator
        DECI num3,d     ;read and store a decimal number in num3
        ADDA num3,d     ;add the contents of num2 to accumulator
        STOREA sum,d    ;store contents of the accumulator into sum
        DECO sum,d      ;output the contents of sum
        STOP            ;stop the processing
        .END            ;end of the program
```

Page 214   7-22

Status Bits

Status bits allow a program to make a choice.

BRLT   Set the PC to the operand, if N is 1

        (A register is *less than* zero)

BREQ   Set the PC to operand, if Z is 1

        (A register is *equal to* zero)

7-23

Testing

- **Test plan** A document that specifies how many times and with what data the program must be run in order to thoroughly test the program

- A **code-coverage** approach designs test cases to ensure that each statement in the program is executed.

- A **data-coverage** approach designs test cases to ensure that the limits of the allowable data are covered.

7-24

Notes

Chapter 8
High-Level Programming Languages

Chapter Goals

- Describe the translation process and distinguish between assembly, compilation, interpretation, and execution
- Name four distinct programming paradigms and name a language characteristic of each
- Describe the following constructs: stream input and output, selection, looping, and subprograms
- Construct Boolean expressions and describe how they are used to alter the flow of control of an algorithm

8-2

Chapter Goals

- Define the concepts of a data type and strong typing
- Explain the concept of a parameter and distinguish between value and reference parameters
- Describe two composite data-structuring mechanisms
- Name, describe, and give examples of the three essential ingredients of an object-oriented language

8-3

Notes

Compilers

- **Compiler** A program that translates a high-level language program into machine code
- High-level languages provide a richer set of instructions that makes the programmer's life even easier

8-4

Compilers

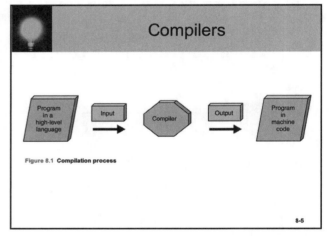

Figure 8.1 **Compilation process**

8-5

Interpreters

- **Interpreter** A translating program that translates and executes the statements in sequence
  - Unlike an assembler or compiler which produce machine code as output, which is then executed in a separate step
  - An interpreter translates a statement and then immediately executes the statement
  - Interpreters can be viewed as *simulators*

8-6

Java

- Introduced in 1996 and swept the computing community by storm
- Portability was of primary importance
- Java is compiled into a standard machine language called **Bytecode**
- A software interpreter called the JVM (Java Virtual Machine) takes the Bytecode program and executes it

8-7

Programming Language Paradigms

- *What is a paradigm*?
- A set of assumptions, concepts, values, and practices that constitute a way of viewing reality

8-8

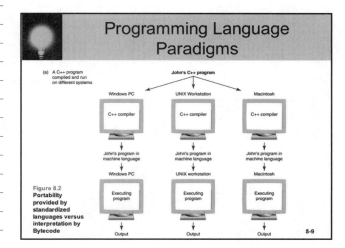

Programming Language Paradigms

(a) A C++ program compiled and run on different systems

John's C++ program

Windows PC — UNIX Workstation — Macintosh

C++ compiler | C++ compiler | C++ compiler

John's program in machine language | John's program in machine language | John's program in machine language

Windows PC | UNIX workstation | Macintosh

Executing program | Executing program | Executing program

Output | Output | Output

Figure 8.2
Portability provided by standardized languages versus interpretation by Bytecode

8-9

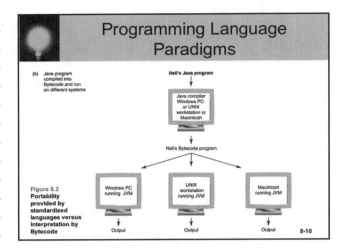

Programming Language Paradigms

(b) Java program compiled into Bytecode and run on different systems

Nell's Java program

Java compiler Windows PC or UNIX workstation or Macintosh

Nell's Bytecode program

Windows PC running JVM

UNIX workstation running JVM

Macintosh running JVM

Figure 8.2 Portability provided by standardized languages versus interpretation by Bytecode

Output   Output   Output

8-10

Programming Language Paradigms

- Imperative or procedural model
  - FORTRAN, COBOL, BASIC, C, Pascal, Ada, and C++

- Functional model
  - LISP, Scheme (a derivative of LISP), and ML

8-11

Programming Language Paradigms

- Logic programming
  - PROLOG

- Object-oriented paradigm
  - SIMULA and Smalltalk
  - C++ is as an imperative language with some object-oriented features
  - Java is an object-oriented language with some imperative features

8-12

Functionality of Imperative Languages

- **Sequence** Executing statements in sequence until an instruction is encountered that changes this sequencing

- **Selection** Deciding which action to take

- **Iteration** (looping) Repeating an action

    Both selection and iteration require the use of a Boolean expression

8-13

Boolean Expressions

- **Boolean expression** A sequence of identifiers, separated by compatible operators, that evaluates to *true* or *false*

- Boolean expression can be
    - A Boolean variable
    - An arithmetic expression followed by a relational operator followed by an arithmetic expression
    - A Boolean expression followed by a Boolean operator followed by a Boolean expression

8-14

Boolean Expressions

- **Variable** A location in memory that is referenced by an identifier that contains a data value

    Thus, a Boolean variable is a location in memory that can contain either *true* or *false*

8-15

Notes

_____
_____
_____
_____
_____
_____
_____
_____
_____
_____
_____
_____
_____
_____
_____
_____
_____
_____
_____
_____
_____
_____
_____
_____
_____
_____
_____
_____
_____
_____
_____
_____
_____
_____
_____
_____
_____

Boolean Expressions

- A relational operator between two arithmetic expressions is asking if the relationship exists between the two expressions

- For example, *xValue < yValue*

Relationship	Symbol
equal to	= or ==
not equal to	<> or != or /=
less than or equal to	<=
greater than or equal to	>=
less than	<
greater than	>

Page 233

8-16

Strong Typing

- **Strong typing** The requirement that only a value of the proper type can be stored into a variable

- **Data type** A description of the set of values and the basic set of operations that can be applied to values of the type

8-17

Data Types

- Integer numbers

- Real numbers

- Characters

- Boolean values

- Strings

8-18

Integers

- The range varies depending upon how many bytes are assigned to represent an integer value

- Some high-level languages provide several integer types of different sizes

- Operations that can be applied to integers are the standard arithmetic and relational operations

8-19

Reals

- Like the integer data type, the range varies depending on the number of bytes assigned to represent a real number

- Many high-level languages have two sizes of real numbers

- The operations that can be applied to real numbers are the same as those that can be applied to integer numbers

8-20

Characters

- It takes one byte to represent characters in the ASCII character set

- Two bytes to represent characters in the Unicode character set

- Our English alphabet is represented in ASCII, which is a subset of Unicode

8-21

Notes

Characters

- Applying arithmetic operations to characters doesn't make much sense
- Comparing characters does make sense, so the relational operators can be applied to characters
- The meaning of "less than" and "greater than" when applied to characters is "comes before" and "comes after" in the character set

8-22

Boolean

- The Boolean data type consists of two values: *true* and *false*
- Not all high-level languages support the Boolean data type
- If a language does not, then you can simulate Boolean values by saying that the Boolean value *true* is represented by 1 and *false* is represented by 0

8-23

Strings

- A string is a sequence of characters considered as one data value
- For example: ***"This is a string."***
  - Containing 17 characters: one uppercase letter, 12 lowercase letters, three blanks, and a period
- The operations defined on strings vary from language to language
  - They include concatenation of strings and comparison of strings in terms of lexicographic order

8-24

Declarations

- **Declaration** A statement that associates an identifier with a variable, an action, or some other entity within the language that can be given a name so that the programmer can refer to that item by name

8-25

Declarations

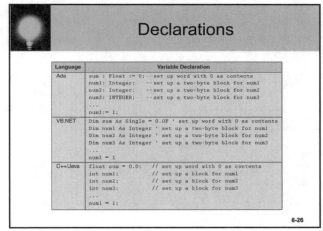

Language	Variable Declaration

Ada	`sum : Float := 0; --set up word with 0 as contents`
	`num1: Integer;   --set up a two-byte block for num1`
	`num2: Integer;   --set up a two-byte block for num2`
	`num3: INTEGER;   --set up a two-byte block for num3`
	`...`
	`num1:= 1;`

VB.NET	`Dim sum As Single = 0.0F ' set up word with 0 as contents`
	`Dim num1 As Integer ' set up a two-byte block for num1`
	`Dim num2 As Integer ' set up a two-byte block for num2`
	`Dim num3 As Integer ' set up a two-byte block for num3`
	`...`
	`num1 = 1`

C++/Java	`float sum = 0.0;    // set up word with 0 as contents`
	`int num1;           // set up a block for num1`
	`int num2;           // set up a block for num2`
	`int num3;           // set up a block for num3`
	`...`
	`num1 = 1;`

8-26

Declarations

- **Reserved word** A word in a language that has special meaning

- **Case-sensitive** Uppercase and lowercase letters are considered the same

8-27

Notes

Assignment statement

- **Assignment statement** An action statement (not a declaration) that says to evaluate the expression on the right-hand side of the symbol and store that value into the place named on the left-hand side

- **Named constant** A location in memory, referenced by an identifier, that contains a data value that cannot be changed

8-28

Assignment Statement

	Constant Declaration

Ada	`Comma    : constant Character := ',';`
	`Message  : constant String := "Hello";`
	`Tax_Rate : constant Float := 8.5;`

VB.NET	`Const WORD1 As Char = ","c`
	`Const MESSAGE As String = "Hello"`
	`Const TaxRate As Double = 8.5`

C++	`const char COMMA = ',';`
	`const string MESSAGE = "Hello";`
	`const double TAX_RATE = 8.5;`

Java	`final char COMMA = ',';`
	`final String MESSAGE = "Hello";`
	`final double TAX_RATE = 8.5;`

Page 238

8-29

Input/Output Structures

- In our pseudocode algorithms we have used the expressions *Read* and *Write*

- High-level languages view input data as a stream of characters divided into lines

8-30

Input/Output Structures

- The key to the processing is in the data type that determines how characters are to be converted to a bit pattern (input) and how a bit pattern is to be converted to characters (output)

- We do not give examples of input/output statements because the syntax is often quite complex and differs so widely among high-level languages

8-31

Control Structures

- **Control structure** An instruction that determines the order in which other instructions in a program are executed

- **Structured programming** A programming methodology in which each logical unit of a program should have just one entry and one exit

- Sequence, selection statements, looping statements, and subprogram statements are control structures

8-32

Selection Statements

- The *if* statement allows the program to test the state of the program variables using a Boolean expression

Language	if Statement

Ada	if Temperature > 75 then
	    Put(Item => "No jacket is necessary")
	else
	    Put (Item => "A light jacket is appropriate");
	end if;

VB.NET	if (Temperature > 75) Then
	    MsgBox("No jacket is necessary")
	Else
	    MsgBox("A light jacket is appropriate")
	End if

C++	if (temperature > 75)
	    cout << "No jacket is necessary";
	else
	    cout << "A light jacket is appropriate";

Java	if (temperature > 75)
	    System.out.print("No jacket is necessary");
	else
	    System.out.print("A light jacket is appropriate");

Page 243

8-33

Notes

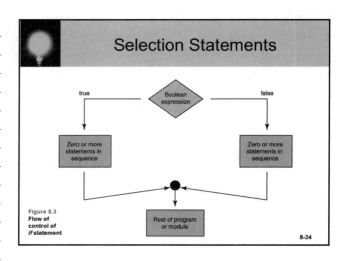

Selection Statements

Figure 8.3
Flow of control of *if* statement

8-34

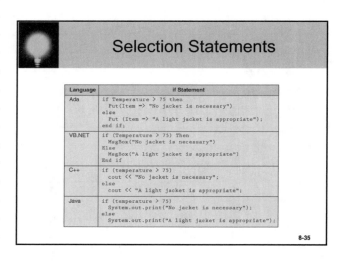

Selection Statements

Language	if Statement

Ada	if Temperature > 75 then
	    Put(Item => "No jacket is necessary")
	else
	    Put (Item => "A light jacket is appropriate");
	end if;

VB.NET	if (Temperature > 75) Then
	    MsgBox("No jacket is necessary")
	Else
	    MsgBox("A light jacket is appropriate")
	End if

C++	if (temperature > 75)
	    cout << "No jacket is necessary";
	else
	    cout << "A light jacket is appropriate";

Java	if (temperature > 75)
	    System.out.print("No jacket is necessary");
	else
	    System.out.print("A light jacket is appropriate");

8-35

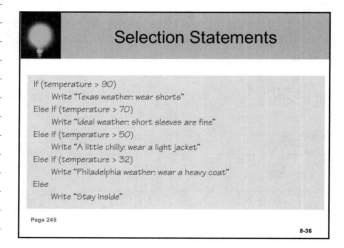

Selection Statements

If (temperature > 90)
    Write "Texas weather: wear shorts"
Else If (temperature > 70)
    Write "Ideal weather: short sleeves are fine"
Else if (temperature > 50)
    Write "A little chilly: wear a light jacket"
Else If (temperature > 32)
    Write "Philadelphia weather: wear a heavy coat"
Else
    Write "Stay inside"

Page 245

8-36

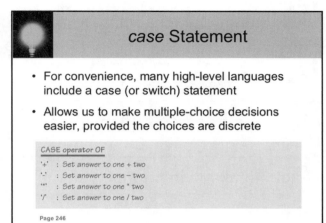

case Statement

- For convenience, many high-level languages include a case (or switch) statement
- Allows us to make multiple-choice decisions easier, provided the choices are discrete

CASE operator OF

'+' : Set answer to one + two
'-' : Set answer to one − two
'*' : Set answer to one * two
'/' : Set answer to one / two

Page 246

8-37

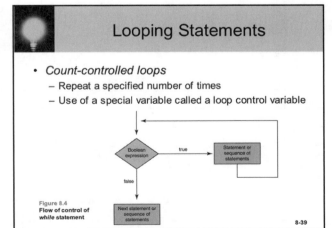

Looping Statements

- The *while* statement is used to repeat a course of action
- Let's look at two distinct types of repetitions

8-38

Looping Statements

- *Count-controlled loops*
  - Repeat a specified number of times
  - Use of a special variable called a loop control variable

Figure 8.4
Flow of control of
while statement

8-39

Notes

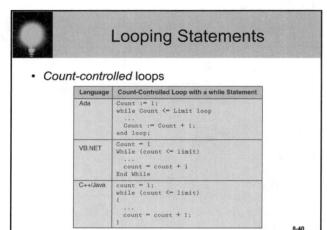

Looping Statements

- *Count-controlled* loops

Language	Count-Controlled Loop with a while Statement

Ada	`Count := 1;`
	`while Count <= Limit loop`
	`    ...`
	`    Count := Count + 1;`
	`end loop;`

VB.NET	`Count = 1`
	`While (count <= limit)`
	`    ...`
	`    count = count + 1`
	`End While`

C++/Java	`count = 1;`
	`while (count <= limit)`
	`{`
	`    ...`
	`    count = count + 1;`
	`}`

8-40

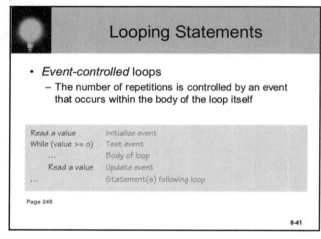

Looping Statements

- *Event-controlled* loops
  - The number of repetitions is controlled by an event that occurs within the body of the loop itself

```
Read a value        Initialize event
While (value >= o)   Test event
    ...              Body of loop
    Read a value     Update event
...                  Statement(s) following loop
```

Page 249

8-41

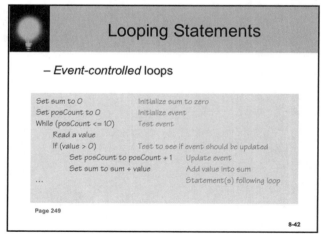

Looping Statements

- *Event-controlled* loops

```
Set sum to 0                    Initialize sum to zero
Set posCount to 0               Initialize event
While (posCount <= 10)          Test event
    Read a value
    If (value > 0)              Test to see if event should be updated
        Set posCount to posCount + 1   Update event
        Set sum to sum + value         Add value into sum
    ...                         Statement(s) following loop
```

Page 249

8-42

Subprogram Statements

- We can give a section of code a name and use that name as a statement in another part of the program

- When the name is encountered, the processing in the other part of the program halts while the named code is executed

8-43

Subprogram Statements

- There are times when the calling unit needs to give information to the subprogram to use in its processing

- A **parameter list** is a list of the identifiers with which the subprogram is to work, along with the types of each identifier placed in parentheses beside the subprogram name

8-44

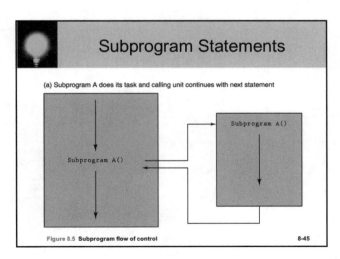

Figure 8.5 **Subprogram flow of control**

8-45

Notes

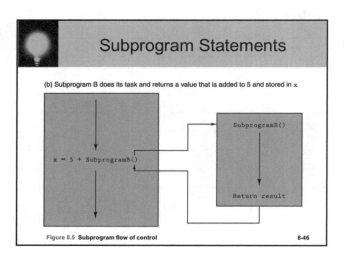

Subprogram Statements

(b) Subprogram B does its task and returns a value that is added to 5 and stored in x

```
x = 5 + SubprogramB()
```

```
SubprogramB()

Return result
```

Figure 8.5 **Subprogram flow of control**

8-46

Subprogram Statements

- **Parameters** Identifiers listed in parentheses beside the subprogram declaration; sometimes they are called formal parameters

- **Arguments** Identifiers listed in parentheses on the subprogram call; sometimes they are called actual parameters

8-47

Subprogram Statements

- **Value parameter** A parameter that expects a copy of its argument to be passed by the calling unit (put on the message board)

- **Reference parameter** A parameter that expects the address of its argument to be passed by the calling unit (put on the message board)

8-48

Chapter 8

Notes

_____

Subprogram Statements

Language	Subprogram Declaration

VB.NET	`Public Sub Example(ByVal one As Integer,`
	`  ByVal two As Integer,`
	`  ByRef three As Single)`
	`...`
	`End Sub`

C++/Java	`void Example(int one; int two; float& three)`
	`{`
	`  ...`
	`}`

Page 253

8-49

Recursion

- **Recursion** The ability of a subprogram to call itself

- Each recursive solution has at least two cases
  - Base case The case to which we have an answer
  - General case The case that expresses the solution in terms of a call to itself with a smaller version of the problem

- For example, the factorial of a number is defined as the number times the product of all the numbers between itself and 0:

$$N! = N * (N - 1)!$$

8-50

Asynchronous Processing

- **Asynchronous processing** The concept that input and output can be accomplished through windows on the screen

  - _Clicking_ has become a major form of input to the computer

  - Mouse clicking is not within the sequence of the program

  - A user can click a mouse at any time during the execution of a program

  - This type of processing is called **asynchronous**

8-51

Composite Data Types

- Records
  - A record is a named *heterogeneous* collection of items in which individual items are accessed by name
  - The elements in the collection can be of various types

8-52

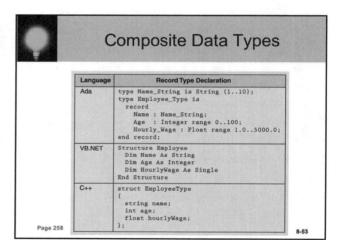

Composite Data Types

Language	Record Type Declaration

Ada	```type Name_String is String (1..10);```
	```type Employee_Type is```
	``` record```
	``` Name : Name_String;```
	``` Age : Integer range 0..100;```
	``` Hourly_Wage : Float range 1.0..5000.0;```
	```end record;```

VB.NET	```Structure Employee```
	``` Dim Name As String```
	``` Dim Age As Integer```
	``` Dim HourlyWage As Single```
	```End Structure```

C++	```struct EmployeeType```
	```{```
	``` string name;```
	``` int age;```
	``` float hourlyWage;```
	```};```

Page 258

8-53

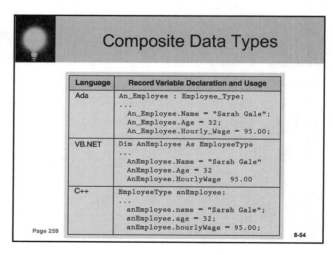

Composite Data Types

Language	Record Variable Declaration and Usage

Ada	```An_Employee : Employee_Type;```
	```...```
	``` An_Employee.Name = "Sarah Gale";```
	``` An_Employee.Age = 32;```
	``` An_Employee.Hourly_Wage = 95.00;```

VB.NET	```Dim AnEmployee As EmployeeType```
	```...```
	``` AnEmployee.Name = "Sarah Gale"```
	``` AnEmployee.Age = 32```
	``` AnEmployee.HourlyWage 95.00```

C++	```EmployeeType anEmployee;```
	```...```
	``` anEmployee.name = "Sarah Gale";```
	``` anEmployee.age = 32;```
	``` anEmployee.hourlyWage = 95.00;```

Page 259

8-54

Notes

Arrays

- An array is a named collection of homogeneous items in which individual items are accessed by their place within the collection
  - The place within the collection is called an *index*

Language	Array Declaration
Ada	type Index_Range is range 1..10; type Ten_Things is array (Index_Range) of Integer;
VB.NET	Dim TenThings(10) As Integer
C++/Java	int tenThings[10];

8-55

Arrays

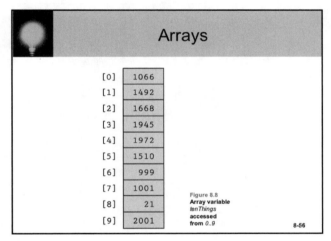

[0]	1066
[1]	1492
[2]	1668
[3]	1945
[4]	1972
[5]	1510
[6]	999
[7]	1001
[8]	21
[9]	2001

Figure 8.8
Array variable
ten Things
accessed
from *0..9*

8-56

Functionality of Object-Oriented Languages

- Encapsulation
- Inheritance
- Polymorphism

8-57

Notes

Encapsulation

- **Encapsulation** A language feature that enforces information hiding

- **Class** A language construct that is a pattern for an object and provides a mechanism for encapsulating the properties and actions of the object class

- **Instantiate** Create an object from a class

8-58

Inheritance

- **Inheritance** A construct that fosters reuse by allowing an application to take an already-tested class and derive a class from it that inherits the properties the application needs

- **Polymorphism** The ability of a language to have duplicate method names in an inheritance hierarchy and to apply the method that is appropriate for the object to which the method is applied

8-59

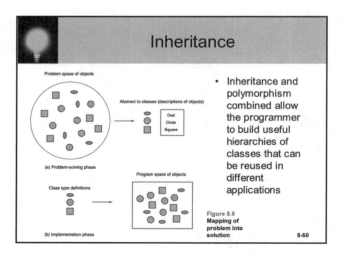

- Inheritance and polymorphism combined allow the programmer to build useful hierarchies of classes that can be reused in different applications

Figure 8.9
Mapping of problem into solution

8-60

Notes

Chapter 9
Abstract Data Types and Algorithms

Computer Science Illuminated
SECOND EDITION
Nell Dale • John Lewis

Chapter Goals

- Define an abstract data type and discuss its role in algorithm development
- Distinguish between a data type and a data structure
- Distinguish between an array-based implementation and a linked implementation
- Distinguish between an array and a list

9-2

Chapter Goals

- Distinguish between an unsorted list and a sorted list
- Distinguish between a selection sort and a bubble sort
- Describe the Quicksort algorithm
- Apply the selection sort, the bubble sort, and the Quicksort to a list of items by hand
- Apply the binary search algorithm

9-3

Chapter Goals

- Distinguish between the behavior of a stack and a queue

- Draw the binary search tree that is built from inserting a series of items

- Demonstrate your understanding of the algorithms in this chapter by hand simulating them with a sequence of items

9-4

Abstract Data Types

- **Abstract data type** A data type whose properties (data and operations) are specified independently of any particular implementation

  The goal in design is to reduce complexity through abstraction

9-5

Abstract Data Types

- In computing, we view data from three perspectives
  - Application level
    - View of the data within a particular problem
  - Logical level
    - An abstract view of the data values (the domain) and the set of operations to manipulate them
  - Implementation level
    - A specific representation of the structure to hold the data items and the coding of the operations in a programming language

9-6

Abstract Data Types

- **Data structures** The implementation of a composite data fields in an abstract data type

- **Containers** Objects whole role is to hold and manipulate other objects

9-7

Array-Based Implementations

- Recall that
  - an array is a named collection of homogeneous items
  - An item's place within the collection is called an index
- If there is no ordering on the items in the container, we call the container unsorted
- If there is an ordering, we call the container sorted

9-8

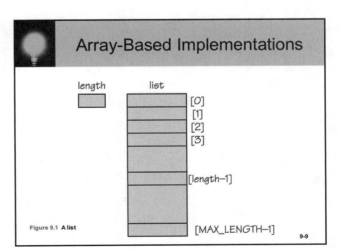

Array-Based Implementations

Figure 9.1 A list

9-9

Notes

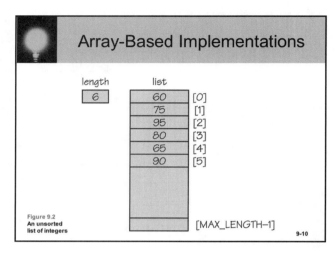

Array-Based Implementations

length   list

| 6 |

60	[0]
75	[1]
95	[2]
80	[3]
65	[4]
90	[5]

[MAX_LENGTH–1]

Figure 9.2
**An unsorted
list of integers**

9-10

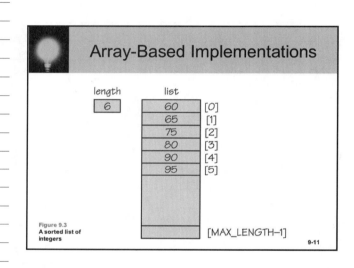

Array-Based Implementations

length   list

| 6 |

60	[0]
65	[1]
75	[2]
80	[3]
90	[4]
95	[5]

[MAX_LENGTH–1]

Figure 9.3
**A sorted list of
integers**

9-11

Linked Implementation

- **Linked implementation** An implementation based on the concept of a *node*

- A node is made up of two pieces of information
  - the item that the user wants in the list, and
  - a pointer to the next node in the list

9-12

Notes

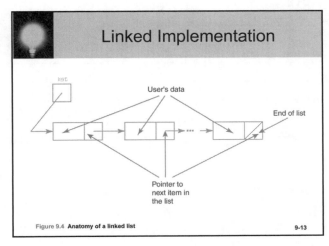

Linked Implementation

User's data

End of list

Pointer to
next item in
the list

Figure 9.4 **Anatomy of a linked list**

9-13

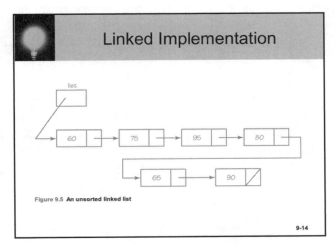

Linked Implementation

list

60 → 75 → 95 → 80

65 → 90

Figure 9.5 **An unsorted linked list**

9-14

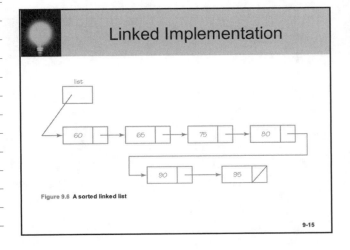

Linked Implementation

list

60 → 65 → 75 → 80

90 → 95

Figure 9.6 **A sorted linked list**

9-15

Notes

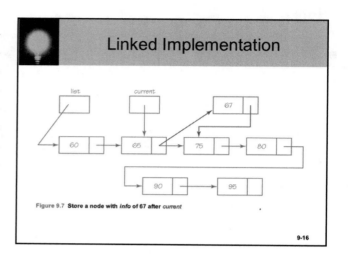

Linked Implementation

Figure 9.7 **Store a node with** *info* **of 67 after** *current*

9-16

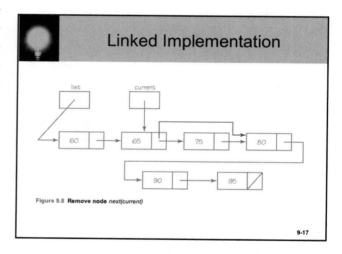

Linked Implementation

Figure 9.8 **Remove node** *next(current)*

9-17

Lists

- List operations
  - Create itself
  - Insert an item
  - Delete an item
  - Print itself
  - Know the number of items it contains
- **Generic data type** (or **class**) A data type or class in which the operations are specified but the type or class of the objects being manipulated is not

9-18

Notes

Sorting

- Because sorting a large number of elements can be extremely time-consuming, a good sorting algorithm is very desirable

- We present several quite different sorting algorithms

9-19

Selection Sort

- List of names
  - Put them in alphabetical order
    - Find the name that comes first in the alphabet, and write it on a second sheet of paper
    - Cross out the name on the original list
    - Continue this cycle until all the names on the original list have been crossed out and written onto the second list, at which point the second list is sorted

9-20

Selection Sort (cont.)

- A slight adjustment to this manual approach does away with the need to duplicate space
  - As you cross a name off the original list, a free space opens up
  - Instead of writing the minimum value on a second list, exchange it with the value currently in the position where the crossed-off item should go

9-21

Notes

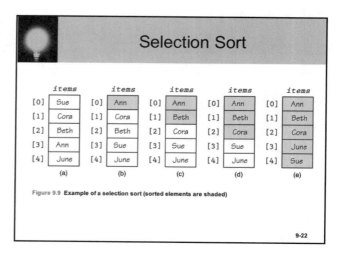

Selection Sort

	items		items		items		items		items
[0]	Sue	[0]	Ann	[0]	Ann	[0]	Ann	[0]	Ann
[1]	Cora	[1]	Cora	[1]	Beth	[1]	Beth	[1]	Beth
[2]	Beth	[2]	Beth	[2]	Cora	[2]	Cora	[2]	Cora
[3]	Ann	[3]	Sue	[3]	Sue	[3]	Sue	[3]	June
[4]	June	[4]	June	[4]	June	[4]	June	[4]	Sue
	(a)		(b)		(c)		(d)		(e)

Figure 9.9 **Example of a selection sort (sorted elements are shaded)**

9-22

Bubble Sort

- A selection sort that uses a different scheme for finding the minimum value
  - Starting with the last list element, we compare successive pairs of elements, swapping whenever the bottom element of the pair is smaller than the one above it

9-23

Bubble Sort

	items		items		items		items		items
[0]	Phil	[0]	Phil	[0]	Phil	[0]	Phil	[0]	Al
[1]	Al	[1]	Al	[1]	Al	[1]	Al	[1]	Phil
[2]	John	[2]	John	[2]	Bob	[2]	Bob	[2]	Bob
[3]	Jim	[3]	Bob	[3]	John	[3]	John	[3]	John
[4]	Bob	[4]	Jim	[4]	Jim	[4]	Jim	[4]	Jim

a) First iteration (Sorted elements are shaded.)

	items		items		items		items
[0]	Al	[0]	Al	[0]	Al	[0]	Al
[1]	Phil	[1]	Bob	[1]	Bob	[1]	Bob
[2]	Bob	[2]	Phil	[2]	Jim	[2]	Jim
[3]	John	[3]	Jim	[3]	Phil	[3]	John
[4]	Jim	[4]	John	[4]	John	[4]	Phil

Figure 9.10
Example of a bubble sort

b) Remaining iterations (Sorted elements are shaded.)

9-24

Notes

Quicksort

- Based on the idea that it is faster and easier to sort two small lists than one larger one
  - Given a large stack of final exams to sort by name
  - Pick a splitting value, say L, and divide the stack of tests into two piles, A–L and M–Z
  - note that the two piles do not necessarily contain the same number of tests
  - Then take the first pile and subdivide it into two piles, A–F and G–L
  - This division process goes on until the piles are small enough to be easily sorted by hand

9-25

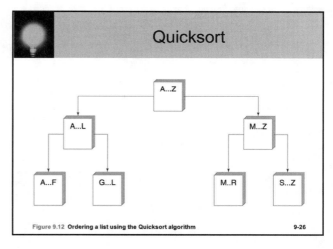

Figure 9.12 **Ordering a list using the Quicksort algorithm**

9-26

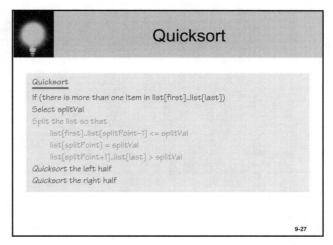

Quicksort

If (there is more than one item in list[first]..list[last])
Select splitVal
Split the list so that
    list[first]..list[splitPoint–1] <= splitVal
    list[splitPoint] = splitVal
    list[splitPoint+1]..list[last] > splitVal
Quicksort the left half
Quicksort the right half

9-27

Notes

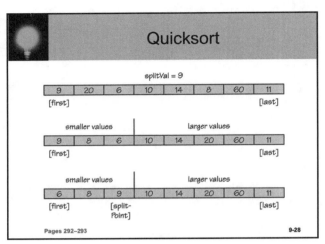

Quicksort

splitVal = 9

| 9 | 20 | 6 | 10 | 14 | 8 | 60 | 11 |

[first]   [last]

smaller values   larger values

| 9 | 8 | 6 | 10 | 14 | 20 | 60 | 11 |

[first]   [last]

smaller values   larger values

| 6 | 8 | 9 | 10 | 14 | 20 | 60 | 11 |

[first]   [split-Point]   [last]

Pages 292–293

9-28

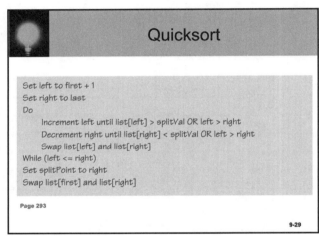

Quicksort

```
Set left to first + 1
Set right to last
Do
    Increment left until list[left] > splitVal OR left > right
    Decrement right until list[right] < splitVal OR left > right
    Swap list[left] and list[right]
While (left <= right)
Set splitPoint to right
Swap list[first] and list[right]
```

Page 293

9-29

Binary Search

- A **sequential search** of a list begins at the beginning of the list and continues until the item is found or the entire list has been searched

- A **binary search** looks for an item in a list using a divide-and-conquer strategy

9-30

Notes

_____

Binary Search

- Binary Search Algorithm
  - Binary search algorithm assumes that the items in the list being searched are sorted
  - The algorithm begins at the middle of the list in a binary search
  - If the item for which we are searching is less than the item in the middle, we know that the item won't be in the second half of the list
  - Once again we examine the "middle" element (which is really the item 25% of the way into the list)
  - The process continues with each comparison cutting in half the portion of the list where the item might be

9-31

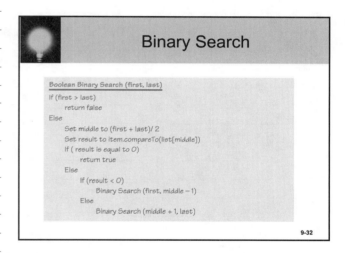

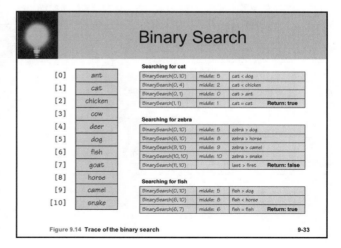

Binary Search

Length	Sequential Search	Binary Search	
		Base 10	Base 2
10	5.5	2.9	3.3
100	50.5	5.8	6.6
1,000	500.5	9.0	9.97
10,000	5000.5	12.0	13.29

Table 9.1 **Average Number of Comparisons**

9-34

Stacks

- A **stack** is an abstract data type in which accesses are made at only one end
  - LIFO, which stands for Last In First Out
  - The insert is called **Push** and the delete is called **Pop**

9-35

Queues

- A **Queue** is an abstract data type in which items are entered at one end and removed from the other end
  - FIFO, for First In First Out
  - Like a waiting line in a bank or supermarket
  - No standard queue terminology
    - **Enqueue, Enque, Enq, Enter,** and **Insert** are used for the insertion operation
    - **Dequeue, Deque, Deq, Delete,** and **Remove** are used for the deletion operation.

9-36

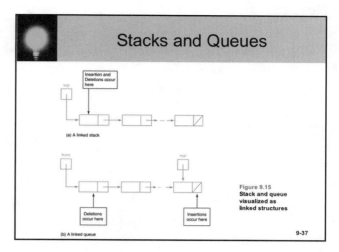

Stacks and Queues

Figure 9.15
Stack and queue visualized as linked structures

(a) A linked stack

(b) A linked queue

9-37

Trees

- ADTs such as lists, stacks, and queues are linear in nature

- More complex relationships require more complex structures

9-38

Trees (cont'd)

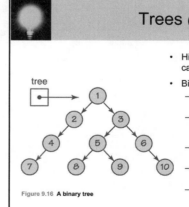

Figure 9.16 **A binary tree**

- Hierarchical structures are called *trees*

- Binary trees
  - Each node has no more than two children
  - The beginning of the tree is a unique starting node called the **root**
  - The node to the left of a node, if it exists, is called its *left child*
  - The node to the right of a node, if it exists, is its *right child*
  - If a node in the tree has no children, it is called a **leaf node**

9-39

Binary Search Trees

- A **binary search tree** has the shape property of a binary tree

- In addition, a binary search tree has a semantic property: The value in any node is greater than the value in any node in its left subtree and less than the value in any node in its right subtree

9-40

Binary Search Tree

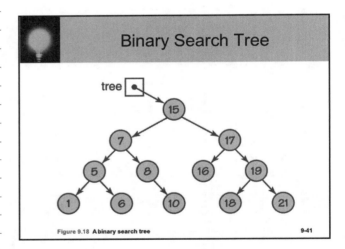

Figure 9.18 A binary search tree

9-41

Binary Search Tree

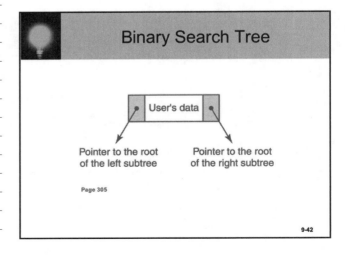

Page 305

9-42

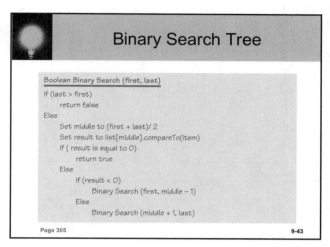

Binary Search Tree

```
Boolean Binary Search (first, last)
If (last > first)
    return false
Else
    Set middle to (first + last)/ 2
    Set result to list[middle].compareTo(item)
    If ( result is equal to O)
        return true
    Else
        If (result < O)
            Binary Search (first, middle – 1)
        Else
            Binary Search (middle + 1, last)
```

Page 305   9-43

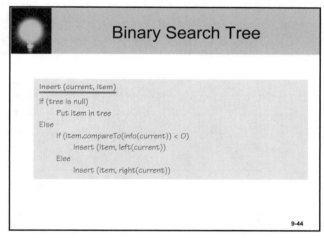

Binary Search Tree

```
Insert (current, item)
If (tree is null)
    Put item in tree
Else
    If (item.compareTo(info(current)) < O)
        Insert (item, left(current))
    Else
        Insert (item, right(current))
```

9-44

Graphs

- **Graph** A data structure that consists of a set of nodes and a set of edges that relate the nodes to each other

- **Undirected graph** A graph in which the edges have no direction

- **Directed graph (Digraph)** A graph in which each edge is directed from one vertex to another (or the same) vertex

9-45

Notes

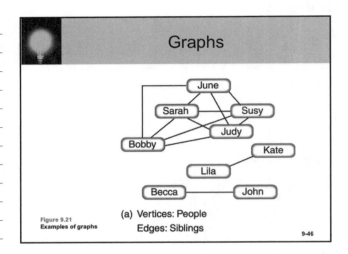

Graphs

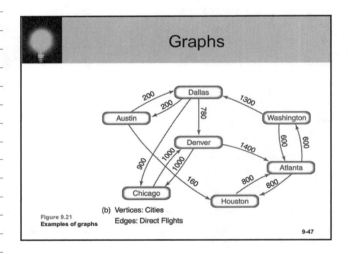

Figure 9.21
Examples of graphs

(a) Vertices: People
Edges: Siblings

9-46

Graphs

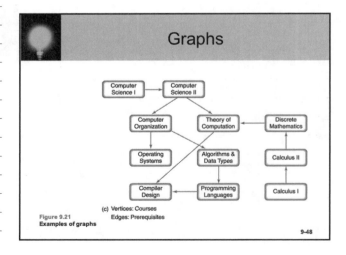

Figure 9.21
Examples of graphs

(b) Vertices: Cities
Edges: Direct Flights

9-47

Graphs

Figure 9.21
Examples of graphs

(c) Vertices: Courses
Edges: Prerequisites

9-48

Chapter 10: Operating Systems

Notes

Computer Science Illuminated
SECOND EDITION
Nell Dale • John Lewis

Chapter 10
Operating Systems

Chapter Goals

- Describe the two main responsibilities of an operating system
- Define memory and process management
- Explain how timesharing creates the virtual machine illusion
- Explain the relationship between logical and physical addresses
- Compare and contrast memory management techniques

10-2

Chapter Goals

- Distinguish between fixed and dynamic partitions
- Define and apply partition selection algorithms
- Explain how demand paging creates the virtual memory illusion
- Explain the stages and transitions of the process life cycle
- Explain the processing of various CPU scheduling algorithms

10-3

Software Categories

- **Application software** Software written to address specific needs—to solve problems in the real world

  Word processing programs, games, inventory control systems, automobile diagnostic programs, and missile guidance programs are all application software

- **System software** Software that manages a computer system at a fundamental level

  It provides the tools and an environment in which application software can be created and run

10-4

Operating System

- An **operating system**
  - manages computer resources, such as memory and input/output devices
  - provides an interface through which a human can interact with the computer
  - allows an application program to interact with these other system resources

10-5

Operating System

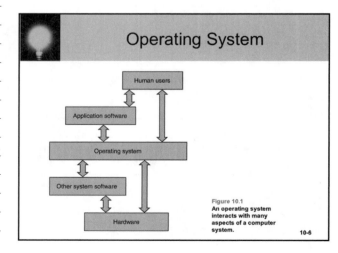

Figure 10.1
An operating system interacts with many aspects of a computer system.

10-6

Operating System

- The various roles of an operating system generally revolve around the idea of "sharing nicely"

- An operating system manages resources, and these resources are often shared in one way or another among programs that want to use them

10-7

Resource Management

- **Multiprogramming** The technique of keeping multiple programs in main memory at the same time that compete for access to the CPU so that they can execute

- **Memory management** The process of keeping track of what programs are in memory and where in memory they reside

10-8

Resource Management

- **Process** A program in execution
- The operating system performs **process management** to carefully track the progress of a process and all of its intermediate states
- **CPU scheduling** determines which process in memory is executed by the CPU at any given point

10-9

Notes

Batch Processing

- A typical computer in the 1960s and '70s was a large machine

- Its processing was managed by a human *operator*

- The operator would organize various jobs from multiple users into *batches*

10-10

Batch Processing

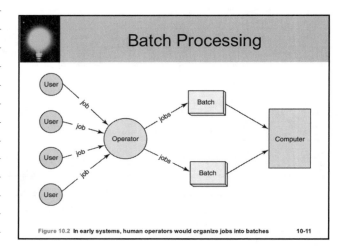

Figure 10.2 In early systems, human operators would organize jobs into batches   10-11

Timesharing

- **Timesharing system** A system that allows multiple users to interact with a computer at the same time

- **Multiprogramming** A technique that allows multiple processes to be active at once, allowing programmers to interact with the computer system directly, while still sharing its resources

- In a timesharing system, each user has his or her own **virtual machine**, in which all system resources are (in effect) available for use

10-12

Other Factors

- **Real-time System** A system in which response time is crucial given the nature of the application

- **Response time** The time delay between receiving a stimulus and producing a response

- **Device driver** A small program that "knows" the way a particular device expects to receive and deliver information.

10-13

Memory Management

- Operating systems must employ techniques to
  - Track where and how a program resides in memory
  - Convert **logical addresses** into actual **addresses**

- **Logical address** (sometimes called a virtual or relative address) A value that specifies a generic location, relative to the program but not to the reality of main memory

- **Physical address** An actual address in the main memory device

10-14

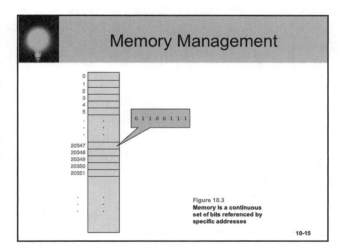

Memory Management

Figure 10.3
Memory is a continuous set of bits referenced by specific addresses

10-15

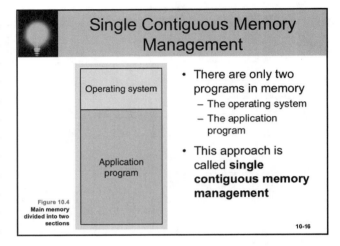

Single Contiguous Memory Management

Figure 10.4
Main memory divided into two sections

Operating system

Application program

- There are only two programs in memory
  - The operating system
  - The application program
- This approach is called **single contiguous memory management**

10-16

Single Contiguous Memory Management

- A logical address is simply an integer value relative to the starting point of the program
- To produce a physical address, we add a logical address to the starting address of the program in physical main memory

10-17

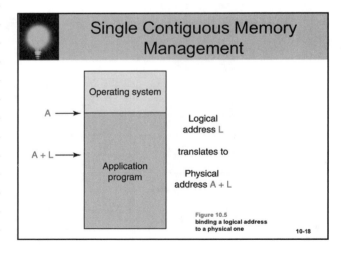

Single Contiguous Memory Management

Operating system

A ⟶

A + L ⟶

Application program

Logical address L

translates to

Physical address A + L

Figure 10.5
binding a logical address to a physical one

10-18

Notes

Partition Memory Management

- **Fixed partitions** Main memory is divided into a particular number of partitions

- **Dynamic partitions** Partitions are created to fit the needs of the programs

10-19

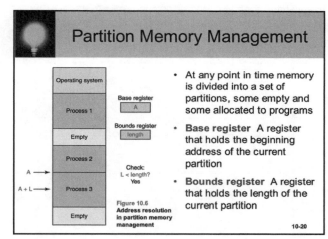

Partition Memory Management

- At any point in time memory is divided into a set of partitions, some empty and some allocated to programs

- **Base register** A register that holds the beginning address of the current partition

- **Bounds register** A register that holds the length of the current partition

Figure 10.6
Address resolution in partition memory management

10-20

Partition Selection Algorithms

Which partition should we allocate to a new program?

- **First fit** Allocate program to the first partition big enough to hold it

- **Best fit** Allocated program to the smallest partition big enough to hold it

- **Worst fit** Allocate program to the largest partition big enough to hold it

10-21

Notes

_____

Paged Memory Management

- **Paged memory technique** A memory management technique in which processes are divided into fixed-size **pages** and stored in memory **frames** when loaded into memory
  - **Frame** A fixed-size portion of _main memory_ that holds a process page
  - **Page** A fixed-size portion of a _process_ that is stored into a memory frame
  - **Page-map table** (PMT) A table used by the operating system to keep track of page/frame relationships

10-22

Paged Memory Management

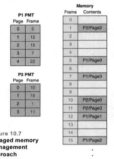

Figure 10.7
A paged memory management approach

- To produce a physical address, you first look up the page in the PMT to find the frame number in which it is stored

- Then multiply the frame number by the frame size and add the offset to get the physical address

10-23

Paged Memory Management

- **Demand paging** An important extension of paged memory management
  - Not all parts of a program actually have to be in memory at the same time
  - In demand paging, the pages are brought into memory on demand

- Page swap The act of bringing in a page from secondary memory, which often causes another page to be written back to secondary memory

10-24

Paged Memory Management

- The demand paging approach gives rise to the idea of **virtual memory,** the illusion that there are no restrictions on the size of a program

- Too much page swapping, however, is called **thrashing** and can seriously degrade system performance.

10-25

Process Management

- The Process States

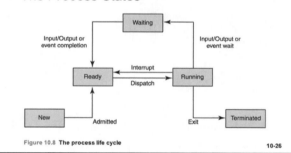

Figure 10.8 **The process life cycle**

10-26

The Process Control Block

- The operating system must manage a large amount of data for each active process

- Usually that data is stored in a data structure called a process control block **(PCB)**

- Each state is represented by a list of PCBs, one for each process in that state

10-27

Notes

The Process Control Block

- Keep in mind that there is only one CPU and therefore only one set of CPU registers
  - These registers contain the values for the currently executing process
- Each time a process is moved to the running state:
  - Register values for the currently running process are stored into its PCB
  - Register values of the new running state are loaded into the CPU
  - This exchange of information is called a **context switch**

10-28

CPU Scheduling

- **CPU Scheduling** The act of determining which process in the *ready* state should be moved to the *running* state
  - Many processes may be in the ready state
  - Only one process can be in the running state, making progress at any one time
- *Which one gets to move from ready to running?*

10-29

CPU Scheduling

- **Nonpreemptive scheduling** The currently executing process gives up the CPU voluntarily
- **Preemptive scheduling** The operating system decides to favor another process, preempting the currently executing process
- **Turnaround time** The amount of time between when a process arrives in the ready state the first time and when it exits the running state for the last time

10-30

CPU Scheduling Algorithms

First-Come, First-Served
– Processes are moved to the CPU in the order in which they arrive in the running state

Shortest Job Next
– Process with shortest estimated running time in the ready state is moved into the running state first

Round Robin
– Each process runs for a specified time slice and moves from the running state to the ready state to await its next turn if not finished

10-31

First-Come, First-Served

Process	Service time
p1	140
p2	75
p3	320
p4	280
p5	125

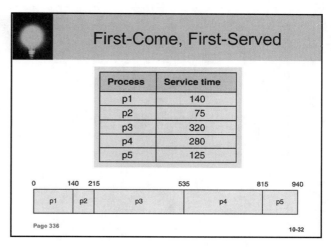

Page 336

10-32

Shortest Job Next

• Looks at all processes in the ready state and dispatches the one with the smallest service time

Page 337

10-33

Round Robin

- Distributes the processing time equitably among all ready processes
- The algorithm establishes a particular **time slice** (or time quantum), which is the amount of time each process receives before being preempted and returned to the ready state to allow another process its turn

10-34

Round Robin

- Suppose the time slice was 50

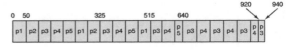

Page 339

10-35

CPU Scheduling Algorithms

Are they preemptive or non-preemptive? Explain

- *First-Come, First-Served?*

- *Shortest Job Next?*

- *Round Robin?*

10-36

Notes

Computer Science
Illuminated
SECOND EDITION
Nell Dale • John Lewis

Chapter 11

File Systems
and Directories

Chapter Goals

- Describe the purpose of files, file systems, and directories
- Distinguish between text and binary files
- Identify various file types by their extensions
- Explain how file types improve file usage
- Define the basic operations on a file

11-2

Chapter Goals

- Compare and contrast sequential and direct file access
- Discuss the issues related to file protection
- Describe a directory tree
- Create absolute and relative paths for a directory tree
- Describe several disk-scheduling algorithms

11-3

File Systems

- **File**   A named collection of related data

- **File system**   The logical view that an operating system provides so that users can manage information as a collection of files

- **Directory**   A named group of files

11-4

Text and Binary Files

- **Text file**   A file in which the bytes of data are organized as characters from the ASCII or Unicode character sets

- **Binary file**   A file that contains data in a specific format, requiring interpretation

11-5

Text and Binary Files

- The terms *text file* and *binary file* are somewhat misleading

- They seem to imply that the information in a text file is not stored as binary data

- Ultimately, all information on a computer is stored as binary digits

- These terms refer to how those bits are formatted: as chunks of 8 or 16 bits, interpreted as characters, or in some other special format

11-6

File Types

- Most files, whether they are in text or binary format, contain a specific type of information

  For example, a file may contain a Java program, a JPEG image, or an MP3 audio clip

- The kind of information contained in a document is called the **file type**

  Most operating systems recognize a list of specific file types

11-7

File Types

Extensions	File type
txt	text data file
mp3, au, wav	audio file
gif, tiff, jpg	image file
doc, wp3	word processing document
java, c, cpp	program source files

Figure 11.1 **Some common file types and their extensions**

- File names are often separated, usually by a period, into two parts
  - Main name
  - File extension
- The **file extension** indicates the type of the file

11-8

File Operations

- Create a file
- Delete a file
- Open a file
- Close a file
- Read data from a file
- Write data to a file
- Reposition the current file pointer in a file

- Append data to the end of a file
- Truncate a file (delete its contents)
- Rename a file
- Copy a file

11-9

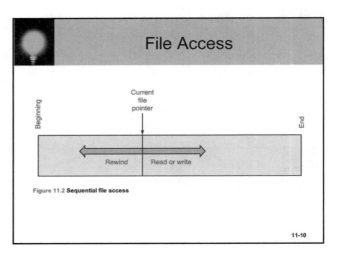

File Access

Current file pointer

Beginning

End

Rewind — Read or write

Figure 11.2 **Sequential file access**

11-10

File Access

- **Sequential access** Information in the file is processed in order, and read and write operations move the current file pointer as far as needed to read or write the data

  The most common file access technique, and the simplest to implement

11-11

File Access

- **Direct access** Files are conceptually divided into numbered logical records and each logical record can be accessed directly by number

11-12

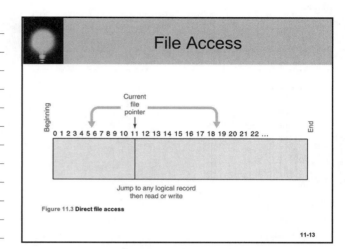

File Access

Current file pointer

Beginning

0 1 2 3 4 5 6 7 8 9 10 11 12 13 14 15 16 17 18 19 20 21 22 ...

End

Jump to any logical record then read or write

Figure 11.3 **Direct file access**

11-13

File Protection

- In multiuser systems, file protection is of primary importance

- We don't want one user to be able to access another user's files unless the access is specifically allowed

- A file protection mechanism determines who can use a file and for what general purpose

11-14

File Protection

- A file's protection settings in the Unix operating system is divided into three categories
  - Owner
  - Group
  - World

	Read	Write/Delete	Execute
Owner	Yes	Yes	No
Group	Yes	No	No
World	No	No	No

Page 356

11-15

Notes

Directory Trees

- A directory of files can be contained within another directory

   The directory containing another is usually called the *parent directory*, and the one inside is called a *subdirectory*

- **Directory tree**   A logical view of a file system; a structure showing the nested directory organization of a file system

- **Root directory**   The directory at the highest level

11-16

Directory Trees

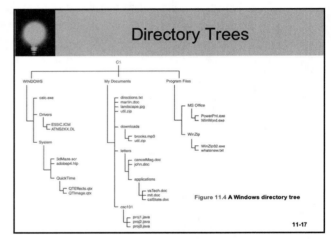

Figure 11.4 **A Windows directory tree**

11-17

Directory Trees

- At any point in time, you can be thought of as working in a particular location (that is, a particular subdirectory)

- **Working directory**   The subdirectory in which you are working

11-18

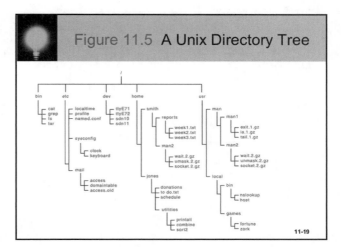

Figure 11.5 A Unix Directory Tree

11-19

Path Names

- **Path** A text designation of the location of a file or subdirectory in a file system, consisting of the series of directories through which you must go to find the file

- **Absolute path** A path that begins at the root and specifies each step down the tree until it reaches the desired file or directory

- **Relative path** A path name that begins at the current working directory

11-20

Path Names

- Examples of absolute path
  C:\Program Files\MS Office\WinWord.exe
  C:\My Documents\letters\applications\vaTech.doc
  C:\Windows\System\QuickTime
- Suppose the current working directory is
  C:\My Documents\letters
- Then the following relative path names could be used
  cancelMag.doc
  applications\calState.doc

11-21

Disk Scheduling

- File systems must be accessed in an efficient manner

- As a computer deals with multiple processes over a period of time, a list of requests to access the disk builds up

- **Disk scheduling** The technique that the operating system uses to determine which requests to satisfy first

11-22

Disk Scheduling

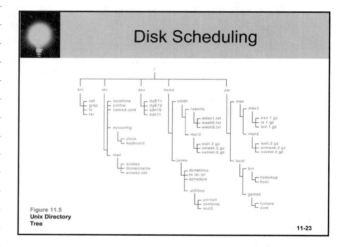

Figure 11.5
Unix Directory Tree

11-23

Disk Scheduling

- **First-Come, First-Served** Requests are serviced in the order they arrive, without regard to the current position of the heads

- **Shortest-seek-time-first** (SSTF) Disk heads are moved the minimum amount possible to satisfy a pending request

- **Scan** Disk heads continuously move in and out servicing requests as they are encountered

11-24

_____

_____

_____

_____

_____

_____

_____

_____

_____

_____

_____

Disk Scheduling

- SCAN Disk Scheduling works like an elevator

  - An elevator is designed to visit floors that have people waiting. In general, an elevator moves from one extreme to the other (say, the top of the building to the bottom), servicing requests as appropriate.

  - The SCAN disk-scheduling algorithm works in a similar way, except instead of moving up and down, the read/write heads move in toward the spindle, then out toward the platter edge, then back toward the spindle, and so forth.

11-25

Notes

Chapter 12

Information Systems

Chapter Goals

- Define the role of general information systems
- Explain how spreadsheets are organized
- Create spreadsheets for basic analysis of data
- Define appropriate spreadsheet formulas using built-in functions
- Design spreadsheets to be flexible and extensible
- Describe the elements of a database management system

12-2

Chapter Goals

- Describe the organization of a relational database
- Establish relationships among elements in a database
- Write basic SQL statements
- Describe an entity-relationship diagram

12-3

Notes

Managing Information

- **Information system** Software that helps us organize and analyze data
  - Flexible application software tools that allow the user to dictate and manage the organization of data, and that have basic processing capabilities to analyze the data in various ways
  - Two of the most popular general application information systems are *electronic spreadsheets* and *database management systems*

12-4

Spreadsheets

- **Spreadsheet** A software application that allows the user to organize and analyze data using a grid of labeled cells
  - A cell can contain data or a formula that is used to calculate a value
  - Data stored in a cell can be text, numbers, or "special" data such as dates
  - Spreadsheet cells are referenced by their row and column designation

	A	B	C	D
1				
2				
3				
4				
5				

Figure 12.1 A spreadsheet, made up of a grid of labeled cells

12-5

Spreadsheets

- Suppose we have collected data on the number of students that came to get help from a set of tutors over a period of several weeks

	A	B	C	D	E	F	G	H
1								
2				Tutor				
3			Hal	Amy	Frank	Total	Avg	
4		1	12	10	13	35	11.67	
5		2	14	16	16	46	15.33	
6	Week	3	10	18	13	41	13.67	
7		4	8	21	18	47	15.67	
8		5	15	18	12	45	15.00	
9		Total	59	83	72	214	71.33	
10		Avg	11.80	16.60	14.40	42.80	14.27	
11								
12								

Figure 12.1
A spreadsheet containing data and computations

12-6

Spreadsheet Formulas

- The power of spreadsheets comes from the formulas that we can create and store in cells
  - When a formula is stored in a cell, the result of the formula is displayed in the cell
  - If we've set up the spreadsheet correctly, we could add or remove tutors, add additional weeks of data, or change any of the data we have already stored and the corresponding calculations would automatically be updated

12-7

Spreadsheet Formulas

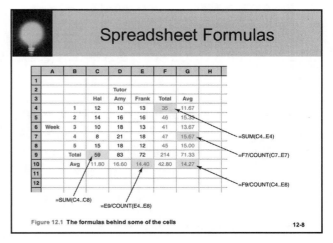

Figure 12.1 **The formulas behind some of the cells**

12-8

Spreadsheet Formulas

- Formulas can make use of basic arithmetic operations using the standard symbols (+, 2, *, and /)
- They can also make use of spreadsheet functions that are built into the software
  - Functions often operate on a set of contiguous cells
- A range of cells is specified with two dots (periods) between the two cell endpoints

12-9

Notes

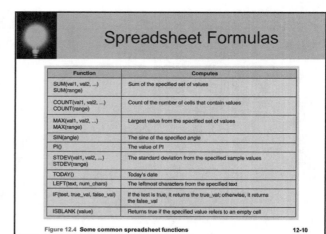

Spreadsheet Formulas

Function	Computes
SUM(val1, val2, ...) SUM(range)	Sum of the specified set of values
COUNT(val1, val2, ...) COUNT(range)	Count of the number of cells that contain values
MAX(val1, val2, ...) MAX(range)	Largest value from the specified set of values
SIN(angle)	The sine of the specified angle
PI()	The value of PI
STDEV(val1, val2, ...) STDEV(range)	The standard deviation from the specified sample values
TODAY()	Today's date
LEFT(text, num_chars)	The leftmost characters from the specified text
IF(test, true_val, false_val)	If the test is true, it returns the true_val; otherwise, it returns the false_val
ISBLANK (value)	Returns true if the specified value refers to an empty cell

Figure 12.4 **Some common spreadsheet functions**

12-10

Circular References

- A circular reference can never be resolved because the result of one formula is ultimately based on another, and vice versa

Cell	Contents
A1	=B7*COUNT(F8..K8)
B7	=A14+SUM(E40..E50)
E45	=G18+G19–D13
D13	=D12/A1

Figure 12.5 **A circular reference situation that cannot be resolved**

12-11

Spreadsheet Analysis

- One reason spreadsheets are so useful is their versatility
- Spreadsheet analysis can be applied to just about any topic area
  - Track sales
  - Analyze sport statistics
  - Maintain student grades
  - Keep a car maintenance log
  - Record and summarize travel expenses
  - Track project activities and schedules
  - Plan stock purchases

12-12

Notes

_____

_____

_____

_____

_____

_____

_____

_____

_____

_____

_____

_____

_____

_____

_____

_____

_____

_____

_____

_____

_____

_____

_____

_____

_____

_____

_____

_____

_____

_____

_____

_____

_____

_____

_____

_____

_____

Spreadsheet Analysis

- Spreadsheets are also useful because of their *dynamic nature*, which provides the powerful ability to do *what-if analysis*

  – *What if the number of attendees decreased by 10%?*

  – *What if we increase the ticket price by $5?*

  – *What if we could reduce the cost of materials by half?*

12-13

Database Management Systems

- **Database** A structured set of data

- **Database management system** (DBMS) A combination of software and data, including a physical database, a database engine, and a database schema
  - **Physical database** A collection of files that contain the data
  - **Database engine** Software that supports access to and modification of the database contents
  - **Database schema** A specification of the logical structure of the data stored in the database

12-14

Database Management Systems

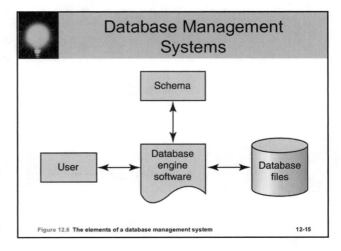

Figure 12.6 **The elements of a database management system**   12-15

Notes

Database Management Systems

- Specialized database languages allow the user to specify the structure of data; add, modify, and delete data; and **query** the database to retrieve specific stored data

- The database **schema** provides the logical view of the data in the database

12-16

The Relational Model

- In a relational DBMS, the data items and the relationships among them are organized into **tables**

  - A table is a collection of **records**

  - A record is a collection of related **fields**

  - Each field of a database table contains a single data value

  - Each record in a table contains the same fields

12-17

A Database Table

Movie

MovieId	Title	Genre	Rating
101	Sixth Sense, The	thriller horror	PG-13
102	Back to the Future	comedy adventure	PG
103	Monsters, Inc.	animation comedy	G
104	Field of Dreams	fantasy drama	PG
105	Alien	sci-fi horror	R
106	Unbreakable	thriller	PG-13
107	X-Men	action sci-fi	PG-13
5022	Elizabeth	drama period	R
5793	Independence Day	action sci-fi	PG-13
7442	Platoon	action drama war	R

Figure 12.7 A database table, made up of records and fields

12-18

A Database Table

- We can express the schema for this part of the database as follows:

  Movie (MovieId:key, Title, Genre, Rating)

12-19

Relationships

Customer

CustomerId	Name	Genre	CreditCardNumber
101	Dennis Cook	123 Main Street	2736 2371 2344 0382
102	Doug Nickle	456 Second Ave	7362 7486 5957 3638
103	Randy Wolf	789 Elm Street	4253 4773 6252 4436
104	Amy Stevens	321 Yellow Brick Road	9876 5432 1234 5678
105	Robert Person	654 Lois Lane	1122 3344 5566 7788
106	David Coggin	987 Broadway	8473 9687 4847 3784
107	Susan Klaton	345 Easy Street	2435 4332 1567 3232

Figure 12.8 **A database table containing customer data**

12-20

Relationships

- We can use a table to represent a collection of relationships between objects

Rents

CustomerId	MovieId	DateRented	DateDue
103	104	3-12-2002	3-13-2002
103	5022	3-12-2002	3-13-2002
105	107	3-12-2002	3-15-2002

Figure 12.9 **A database table storing current movie rentals**

12-21

Structured Query Language

- **Structured Query Language (SQL)** A comprehensive database language for managing relational databases

12-22

Queries in SQL

select *attribute-list* from *table-list* where *condition*

select Title from Movie where Rating = 'PG'

select Name, Address from Customer

select * from Movie where Genre like '%action%'

select * from Movie where Rating = 'R' order by Title

12-23

Modifying Database Content

insert into Customer values (9876, 'John Smith', '602 Greenbriar Court', '2938 3212 3402 0299')

update Movie set Genre = 'thriller drama' where title = 'Unbreakable'

delete from Movie where Rating = 'R'

12-24

Notes

Database Design

- **Entity-relationship (ER) modeling** A popular technique for designing relational databases

- **ER Diagram** Chief tool used for ER modeling that captures the important record types, attributes, and relationships in a graphical form

12-25

Database Design

- These designations show the **cardinality constraint** of the relationship

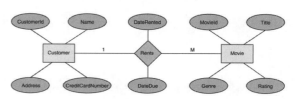

Figure 12.10 **An ER diagram for the movie rental database**

12-26

Notes

Computer Science Illuminated
SECOND EDITION
Nell Dale • John Lewis

Chapter 13
Artificial Intelligence

Chapter Goals

- Distinguish between the types of problems that humans do best and those that computers do best

- Explain the Turing test

- Define what is meant by knowledge representation and demonstrate how knowledge is represented in a semantic network

13-2

Chapter Goals

- Develop a search tree for simple scenarios
- Explain the processing of an expert system
- Explain the processing of biological and artificial neural networks
- List the various aspects of natural language processing
- Explain the types of ambiguities in natural language comprehension

13-3

Thinking Machines

- A computer can do some things better -- and certainly faster--than a human can
  - Adding a thousand four-digit numbers
  - Counting the distribution of letters in a book
  - Searching a list of 1,000,000 numbers for duplicates
  - Matching finger prints

13-4

Thinking Machines

Figure 13.1 **A computer might have trouble identifying the cat in this picture.**

- BUT a computer would have difficulty pointing out the cat in this picture, which is easy for a human

- **Artificial intelligence** (AI) The study of computer systems that attempt to model and apply the intelligence of the human mind

13-5

The Turing Test

- In 1950 English mathematician Alan Turing wrote a landmark paper that asked the question: *Can machines think?*

- How will we know when we've succeeded?

- The **Turing test** is used to empirically determine whether a computer has achieved intelligence

13-6

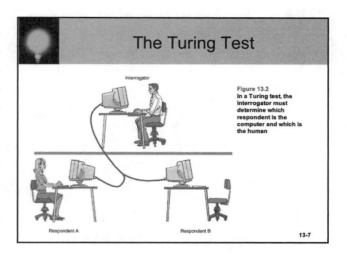

The Turing Test

Interrogator

Figure 13.2
In a Turing test, the interrogator must determine which respondent is the computer and which is the human

Respondent A

Respondent B

13-7

The Turing Test

- **Weak equivalence** Two systems (human and computer) are equivalent in results (output), but they do not arrive at those results in the same way

- **Strong equivalence** Two systems (human and computer) use the same internal processes to produce results

13-8

Knowledge Representation

- The knowledge needed to represent an object or event depends on the situation

- There are many ways to represent knowledge
  - Natural language
  - Though natural language is very descriptive, it doesn't lend itself to efficient processing

13-9

Notes

Semantic Networks

- **Semantic network** A knowledge representation technique that focuses on the relationships between objects

- A directed graph is used to represent a semantic network or net

13-10

Semantic Networks

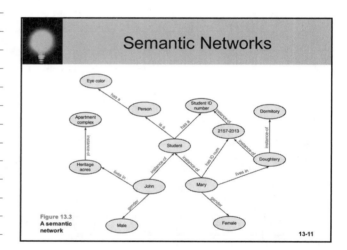

Figure 13.3
A semantic network

13-11

Semantic Networks

- The relationships that we represent are completely our choice, based on the information we need to answer the kinds of questions that we will face

- The types of relationships represented determine which questions are easily answered, which are more difficult to answer, and which cannot be answered

13-12

Notes

Search Trees

- **Search tree** A structure that represents all possible moves in a game, for both you and your opponent

- The paths down a search tree represent a series of decisions made by the players

13-13

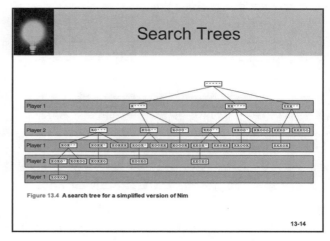

Figure 13.4 **A search tree for a simplified version of Nim**

13-14

Search Trees

- Search tree analysis can be applied nicely to other, more complicated games such as chess

- Because these trees are so large, only a fraction of the tree can be analyzed in a reasonable time limit, even with modern computing power

13-15

Notes

_____

Search Trees

Techniques for searching trees

- **Depth-first** A technique that involves the analysis of selected paths all the way down the tree

- **Breadth-first** A technique that involves the analysis of all possible paths but only for a short distance down the tree

Breadth-first tends to yield the best results

13-16

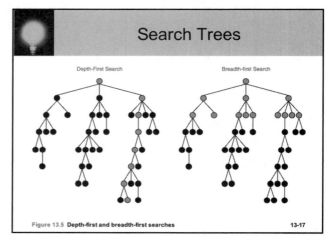

Search Trees

Depth-First Search   Breadth-first Search

Figure 13.5 **Depth-first and breadth-first searches**   13-17

Expert Systems

- **Knowledge-based system** A software system that embodies and uses a specific set of information from which it extracts and processes particular pieces

- **Expert system** A software system based the knowledge of human experts in a specialized field
  - An expert system uses a set of rules to guide its processing
  - The inference engine is the part of the software that determines how the rules are followed

13-18

Notes

Expert Systems

- Example: What type of treatment should I put on my lawn?
  - NONE—apply no treatment at this time
  - TURF—apply a turf-building treatment
  - WEED—apply a weed-killing treatment
  - BUG—apply a bug-killing treatment
  - FEED—apply a basic fertilizer treatment
  - WEEDFEED—apply a weed-killing and fertilizer combination treatment

13-19

Expert Systems

- Boolean variables
  - BARE—the lawn has large, bare areas
  - SPARSE—the lawn is generally thin
  - WEEDS—the lawn contains many weeds
  - BUGS—the lawn shows evidence of bugs

13-20

Expert Systems

- Some rules
  - if (CURRENT – LAST < 30) then NONE
  - if (SEASON = winter) then not BUGS
  - if (BARE) then TURF
  - if (SPARSE and not WEEDS) then FEED
  - if (BUGS and not SPARSE) then BUG
  - if (WEEDS and not SPARSE) then WEED
  - if (WEEDS and SPARSE) then WEEDFEED

13-21

Notes

Expert Systems

- An execution of our inference engine
  - System: Does the lawn have large, bare areas?
  - User: No
  - System: Does the lawn show evidence of bugs?
  - User: No
  - System: Is the lawn generally thin?
  - User: Yes
  - System: Does the lawn contain significant weeds?
  - User: Yes
  - System: You should apply a weed-killing and fertilizer combination treatment.

13-22

Artificial Neural Network

- Attempts to mimic the actions of the neural networks of the human body

- Let's first look at how a biological neural network works
  - A neuron is a single cell that conducts a chemically-based electronic signal
  - At any point in time a neuron is in either an excited or inhibited state

13-23

Artificial Neural Network

  - A series of connected neurons forms a pathway
  - A series of excited neurons creates a strong pathway
  - A biological neuron has multiple input tentacles called dendrites and one primary output tentacle called an axon
  - The gap between an axon and a dendrite is called a synapse

13-24

Notes

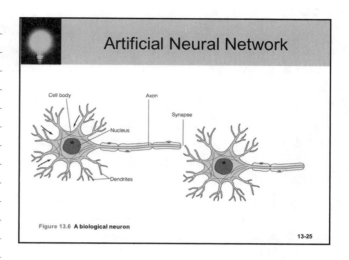

Artificial Neural Network

Cell body

Axon

Synapse

Nucleus

Dendrites

Figure 13.6 **A biological neuron**

13-25

Artificial Neural Network

- A neuron accepts multiple input signals and then controls the contribution of each signal based on the "importance" the corresponding synapse gives to it

- The pathways along the neural nets are in a constant state of flux

- As we learn new things, new strong neural pathways in our brain are formed

13-26

Artificial Neural Networks

- Each processing element in an artificial neural net is analogous to a biological neuron
  - An element accepts a certain number of input values and produces a single output value of either 0 or 1
  - Associated with each input value is a numeric weight

13-27

Notes

Artificial Neural Networks

- The **effective weight** of the element is defined to be the sum of the weights multiplied by their respective input values

  $v1*w1 + v2*w2 + v3*w3$

- Each element has a numeric threshold value

- If the effective weight exceeds the threshold, the unit produces an output value of 1

- If it does not exceed the threshold, it produces an output value of 0

13-28

Artificial Neural Networks

- The process of adjusting the weights and threshold values in a neural net is called **training**

- A neural net can be trained to produce whatever results are required

13-29

Natural Language Processing

- There are three basic types of processing going on during human/computer voice interaction
  - Voice recognition—recognizing human words
  - Natural language comprehension—interpreting human communication
  - Voice synthesis—recreating human speech

- Common to all of these problems is the fact that we are using a natural language, which can be any language that humans use to communicate

13-30

Voice Synthesis

- There are two basic approaches to the solution
  - Dynamic voice generation
  - Recorded speech
- **Dynamic voice generation** A computer examines the letters that make up a word and produces the sequence of sounds that correspond to those letters in an attempt to vocalize the word
- **Phonemes** The sound units into which human speech has been categorized

13-31

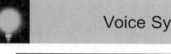

Voice Synthesis

Consonants				Vowels	
Symbols	Examples	Symbols	Examples	Symbols	Examples
p	pipe	k	kick, cat	i	eel, sea, see
b	babe	g	get	I	ill, bill
m	maim	ŋ	sing	e	ale, aim, day
f	fee, phone, rough	š	shoe, ash, sugar	ɛ	elk, bet, bear
v	vie, love	ž	measure	æ	at, mat
θ	thin, bath	č	chat, batch	u	due, new, zoo
ð	the, bathe	j	jaw, judge, gin	ʊ	book, sugar
t	tea, beat	d	day, bad	o	own, no, know
n	nine	ʔ	uh uh	ɔ	aw, crawl, law, dog
l	law, ball	s	see, less, city	a	hot, bar, dart
r	run, bar	z	zoo, booze	ə	sir, nerd, bird
				ʌ	cut, bun

Semi Vowels	
w	we
h	he
j	you, beyond

Dipthongs	
aj	bite, fight
aw	out, cow
ɔj	boy, boil

Figure 13.7 **Phonemes for American English**

13-32

Voice Synthesis

- **Recorded speech** A large collection of words is recorded digitally and individual words are selected to make up a message

Telephone voice mail systems often use this approach: "Press 1 to leave a message for Nell Dale; press 2 to leave a message for John Lewis."

13-33

Notes

Voice Synthesis

- Each word or phrase needed must be recorded separately
- Furthermore, since words are pronounced differently in different contexts, some words may have to be recorded multiple times
  - For example, a word at the end of a question rises in pitch compared to its use in the middle of a sentence

13-34

Voice Recognition

- The sounds that each person makes when speaking are unique
- We each have a unique shape to our mouth, tongue, throat, and nasal cavities that affect the pitch and resonance of our spoken voice
- Speech impediments, mumbling, volume, regional accents, and the health of the speaker further complicate this problem

13-35

Voice Recognition

- Furthermore, humans speak in a continuous, flowing manner
  - Words are strung together into sentences
  - Sometimes it's difficult to distinguish between phrases like "ice cream" and "I scream"
  - Also, homonyms such as "I" and "eye" or "see" and "sea"
- Humans can often clarify these situations by the context of the sentence, but that processing requires another level of comprehension
- Modern voice-recognition systems still do not do well with continuous, conversational speech

13-36

Natural Language Comprehension

- Even if a computer recognizes the words that are spoken, it is another task entirely to understand the *meaning* of those words
  - Natural language is inherently ambiguous, meaning that the same syntactic structure could have multiple valid interpretations
  - A single word can have multiple definitions and can even represent multiple parts of speech
  - This is referred to as a lexical ambiguity

  Time flies like an arrow.

13-37

Natural Language Comprehension

- A natural language sentence can also have a syntactic ambiguity because phrases can be put together in various ways

  I saw the Grand Canyon flying to New York.

- Referential ambiguity can occur with the use of pronouns

  The brick fell on the computer but it is not broken.

13-38

Robotics

- **Mobile robotics** The study of robots that move relative to their environment, while exhibiting a degree of autonomy

- In the **sense-plan-act (SPA) paradigm** the world of the robot is represented in a complex semantic net in which the sensors on the robot are used to capture the data to build up the net

Figure 13.8 **The sense-plan-act (SPA) paradigm**

13-39

Subsumption Architecture

- Rather than trying to model the entire world all the time, the robot is given a simple set of behaviors each associated with the part of the world necessary for that behavior

Figure 13.9
The new control paradigm

13-40

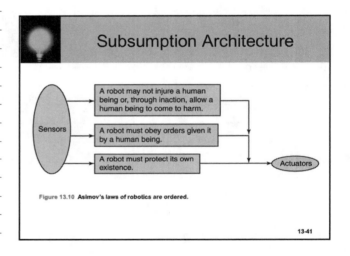

Subsumption Architecture

Figure 13.10 **Asimov's laws of robotics are ordered.**

13-41

Notes

Computer Science Illuminated
SECOND EDITION
Nell Dale • John Lewis

Chapter 14

Simulation and Other Applications

Chapter Goals

- Define simulation
- Give examples of complex systems
- Distinguish between continuous and discrete event simulation
- Explain how object-oriented design principles can be used in building models

14-2

Chapter Goals

- Name and discuss the four parts of a queuing system
- Explain the complexity of weather and seismic models
- Explain the concept of embedded systems and give examples from your own home
- Distinguish between two-dimensional and three-dimensional CAD systems

14-3

What Is Simulation?

- **Simulation** A model of a complex system and the experimental manipulation of the model to observe the results

  Systems that are best suited to being simulated are *dynamic*, *interactive*, and *complicated*

- **Model** An abstraction of a real system

  It is a representation of the objects within the system and the rules that govern the interactions of the objects

14-4

Constructing Models

- Continuous simulation

  – Treats time as continuous and expresses changes in terms of a set of differential equations that reflect the relationships among the set of characteristics

  – Meteorological models falls into this category

14-5

Constructing Models

- Discrete event simulation

  – Made up of *entities, attributes,* and *events*

  – Entity The representation of some object in the real system that must be explicitly defined

  – Attribute Some characteristic of a particular entity

  – Event An interaction between entities

14-6

Notes

Queuing Systems

- **Queuing system** A discrete-event model that uses random numbers to represent the arrival and duration of events
  - The system is made up of servers and queues of objects to be served
  - The objective is to utilize the servers as fully as possible while keeping the wait time within a reasonable limit

14-7

Queuing Systems

- To construct a queuing model, we must know the following four things
  - The number of events and how they affect the system in order to determine the rules of entity interaction
  - The number of servers
  - The distribution of arrival times in order to determine if an entity enters the system
  - The expected service time in order to determine the duration of an event

14-8

Meteorological Models

- Meteorological models are based on the time-dependent partial differential equations of fluid mechanics and thermodynamics

- Initial values for the variables are entered from observation, and the equations are solved to define the values of the variables at some later time

14-9

Meteorological Models

- Computer models are designed to aid the weathercaster, not replace him or her

    – The outputs from the computer models are predictions of the values of variables in the future

    – It is up to the weathercaster to determine what the values *mean*

14-10

Hurricane Tracking

- The modules for hurricane tracking are called *relocatable* models, because they are applied to a moving target

- The Geophysical and Fluid Dynamics Laboratory (GFDL) developed the most recent hurricane model in order to improve the prediction of where a hurricane would make landfall

14-11

Hurricane Tracking

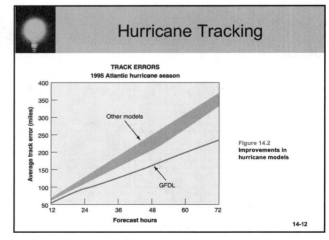

Figure 14.2
Improvements in hurricane models

14-12

Notes

Graphics and Computer-Aided Design (CAD)

- Graphics is the language of communications for engineers, designers, and architects

- Computer-aided design (CAD)   A system that uses computers with advanced graphics hardware and software to create precision drawings or technical illustrations

14-13

Graphics and Computer-Aided Design (CAD)

- CAD systems can be broadly classified as two-dimensional (2-D) CAD and three-dimensional (3-D) CAD

- There are three methods of modeling in three dimensions
  - Wireframe modeling
  - Surface modeling
  - Solid modeling

14-14

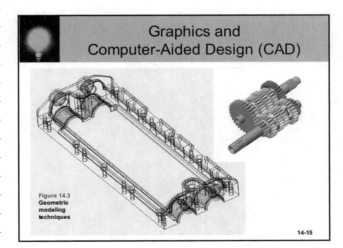

Graphics and Computer-Aided Design (CAD)

Figure 14.3
Geometric modeling techniques

14-15

Embedded Systems

- Embedded systems are computers that are dedicated to perform a narrow range of functions as part of a larger system

  - Typically, an embedded system is housed on a single microprocessor chip with the programs stored in ROM

  - Virtually all appliances that have a digital interface—watches, microwaves, VCRs, cars—utilize embedded systems

  - In fact, the term *embedded system* is nebulous because it encompasses about everything except desktop PCs

14-16

Notes

Computer Science
Illuminated
SECOND EDITION
Nell Dale • John Lewis

Chapter 15

Networks

Chapter Goals

- Describe the core issues related to computer networks
- List various types of networks and their characteristics
- Explain various topologies of local-area networks
- Explain why network technologies are best implemented as open systems

15-2

Chapter Goals

- Compare and contrast various technologies for home Internet connections
- Explain packet switching
- Describe the basic roles of various network protocols
- Explain the role of a firewall
- Compare and contrast network hostnames and IP addresses
- Explain the domain name system

15-3

Notes

Networking

- **Computer network** A collection of computing devices that are connected in various ways in order to communicate and share resources

  Usually, the connections between computers in a network are made using physical wires or cables
  - However, some connections are **wireless**, using radio waves or infrared signals

15-4

Networking

- The generic term **node** or **host** refers to any device on a network
- **Data transfer rate** The speed with which data is moved from one place on a network to another
- Data transfer rate is a key issue in computer networks

15-5

Networking

- Computer networks have opened up an entire frontier in the world of computing called the **client/server model**

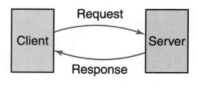

Figure 15.1 Client/Server interaction

15-6

Networking

- **File server** A computer that stores and manages files for multiple users on a network

- **Web server** A computer dedicated to responding to requests (from the browser client) for web pages

15-7

Types of Networks

- **Local-area network (LAN)**   A network that connects a relatively small number of machines in a relatively close geographical area

15-8

Types of Networks

- Various configurations, called topologies, have been used to administer LANs

  - **Ring topology** A configuration that connects all nodes in a closed loop on which messages travel in one direction

  - **Star topology** A configuration that centers around one node to which all others are connected and through which all messages are sent

  - **Bus topology**   All nodes are connected to a single communication line that carries messages in both directions

15-9

Notes

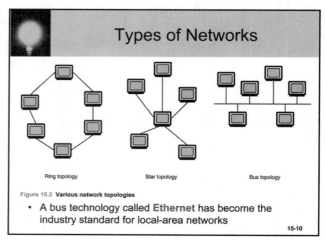

Types of Networks

Ring topology   Star topology   Bus topology

Figure 15.2 **Various network topologies**

- A bus technology called **Ethernet** has become the industry standard for local-area networks

15-10

Types of Networks

- **Wide-area network (WAN)** A network that connects two or more local-area networks over a potentially large geographic distance

  Often one particular node on a LAN is set up to serve as a **gateway** to handle all communication going between that LAN and other networks

  Communication between networks is called internetworking

  The **Internet,** as we know it today, is essentially the ultimate wide-area network, spanning the entire globe

15-11

Types of Networks

- **Metropolitan-area network (MAN)** The communication infrastructures that have been developed in and around large cities

15-12

So, who owns the Internet?

Well, nobody does. No single person or company owns the Internet or even controls it entirely. As a wide-area network, it is made up of many smaller networks. These smaller networks are often owned and managed by a person or organization. The Internet, then, is really defined by how connections can be made between these networks.

15-13

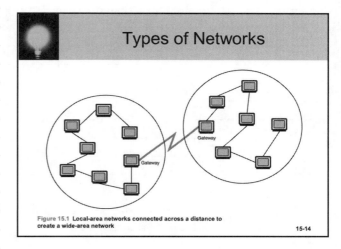

Types of Networks

Figure 15.1 Local-area networks connected across a distance to create a wide-area network

15-14

Internet Connections

- **Internet backbone** A set of high-speed networks that carry Internet traffic

  These networks are provided by companies such as AT&T, GTE, and IBM

- **Internet service provider (ISP)** A company that provides other companies or individuals with access to the Internet

15-15

Internet Connections

- There are various technologies available that you can use to connect a home computer to the Internet
    - A **phone modem** converts computer data into an analog audio signal for transfer over a telephone line, and then a modem at the destination converts it back again into data
    - A **digital subscriber line (DSL)** uses regular copper phone lines to transfer digital data to and from the phone company's central office
    - A **cable modem** uses the same line that your cable TV signals come in on to transfer the data back and forth

15-16

Internet Connections

- **Broadband** A connection in which transfer speeds are faster than 128 bits per second
    - DSL connections and cable modems are broadband connections
    - The speed for **downloads** (getting data from the Internet to your home computer) may not be the same as **uploads** (sending data from your home computer to the Internet)

15-17

Packet Switching

- To improve the efficiency of transferring information over a shared communication line, messages are divided into fixed-sized, numbered **packets**
- Network devices called routers are used to direct packets between networks

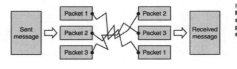

Figure 15.4
Messages sent by packet switching

Message is divided into packets — Packets are sent over the Internet by the most expedient route — Packets are reordered and then reassembled

15-18

Open Systems

- **Proprietary system** A system that uses technologies kept private by a particular commercial vendor
  One system couldn't communicate with another, leading to the need for

- **Interoperability** The ability of software and hardware on multiple machines and from multiple commercial vendors to communicate
  Leading to

- **Open systems** Systems based on a common model of network architecture and a suite of protocols used in its implementation

15-19

Open Systems

7	Application layer
6	Presentation layer
5	Session layer
4	Transport layer
3	Network layer
2	Data Link layer
1	Physical layer

Figure 15.5 **The layers of the OSI Reference Model**

- The International Organization for Standardization (ISO) established the **Open Systems Interconnection (OSI) Reference Model**

- Each layer deals with a particular aspect of network communication

15-20

Network Protocols

- Network protocols are layered such that each one relies on the protocols that underlie it

- Sometimes referred to as a **protocol stack**

SMTP	FTP	Telnet	
Transmission Control Protocol (TCP)		User Datagram Protocol (UDP)	
Internet Protocol (IP)			

Figure 15.6 **Layering of key network protocols**

15-21

Notes

TCP/IP

- TCP stands for **Transmission Control Protocol**

  TCP software breaks messages into packets, hands them off to the IP software for delivery, and then orders and reassembles the packets at their destination

- IP stands for **Internet Protocol**

  IP software deals with the routing of packets through the maze of interconnected networks to their final destination

15-22

TCP/IP (cont.)

- UDP stands for **User Datagram Protocol**

  – It is an alternative to TCP

  – The main difference is that TCP is highly reliable, at the cost of decreased performance, while UDP is less reliable, but generally faster

15-23

High-Level Protocols

- Other protocols build on the foundation established by the TCP/IP protocol suite

  – Simple Mail Transfer Protocol (SMTP)

  – File Transfer Protocol (FTP)

  – Telnet

  – Hyper Text Transfer Protocol (http)

15-24

MIME Types

- Related to the idea of network protocols and standardization is the concept of a file's MIME type

  - MIME stands for **Multipurpose Internet Mail Extension**

  - Based on a document's MIME type, an application program can decide how to deal with the data it is given

15-25

MIME Types

Protocol	Port
Echo	7
File Transfer Protocol (FTP)	21
Telnet	23
Simple Mail Transfer Protocol (SMTP)	25
Domain Name Service (DNS)	53
Gopher	70
Finger	79
Hyper Text Transfer Protocol (HTTP)	80
Post Office Protocol (POP3)	110
Network News Transfer Protocol (NNTP)	119
Internet Relay Chat (IRC)	6667

Figure 15.7
Some protocols and the ports they use

15-26

Firewalls

- **Firewall** A machine and its software that serve as a special gateway to a network, protecting it from inappropriate access

  - Filters the network traffic that comes in, checking the validity of the messages as much as possible and perhaps denying some messages altogether

  - Enforces an organization's **access control policy**

15-27

Notes

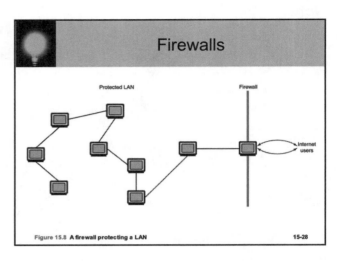

Firewalls

Protected LAN   Firewall

Internet users

Figure 15.8 **A firewall protecting a LAN**   15-28

Network Addresses

- **Hostname** A unique identification that specifies a particular computer on the Internet

  For example
  matisse.csc.villanova.edu
  condor.develocorp.com

  15-29

Network Addresses

- Network software translates a hostname into its corresponding IP address

  For example
  205.39.145.18

  15-30

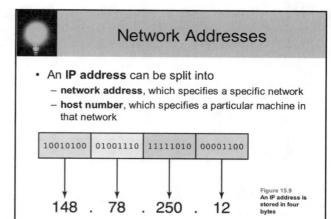

Network Addresses

- An **IP address** can be split into
  - **network address**, which specifies a specific network
  - **host number**, which specifies a particular machine in that network

10010100	01001110	11111010	00001100

148 . 78 . 250 . 12

Figure 15.9
An IP address is stored in four bytes

15-31

Domain Name System

- A hostname consists of the computer name followed by **the domain name**

- csc.villanova.edu is the domain name
  - A domain name is separated into two or more sections that specify the organization, and possibly a subset of an organization, of which the computer is a part
  - Two organizations can have a computer named the same thing because the domain name makes it clear which one is being referred to

15-32

Domain Name System

- The very last section of the domain is called its **top-level domain (TLD)** name

Top-Level Domain	General Purpose	New TLDs	General Purpose
.com	U.S. Commercial	.biz	Business
.net	Network	.info	Information
.org	Nonprofit organization	.pro	Professional
.edu	U.S. Educational	.museum	Museums
.int	International	.aero	Aerospace industry
.mil	U.S. Military	.coop	Cooperative
.gov	U.S. Government		

Figure 15.10 **Top-level domains, including some relatively new ones**

15-33

Notes

Domain Name System

- Organizations based in countries other than the United States use a top-level domain that corresponds to their two-letter country codes

Country Code TLD	Country
.au	Australia
.br	Brazil
.ca	Canada
.gr	Greece
.in	India
.ru	Russian Federation
.uk	United Kingdom

Figure 15.11
Some of the top-level domain names based on country codes

15-34

Domain Name System

- The **domain name system** (DNS) is chiefly used to translate hostnames into numeric IP addresses
  - DNS is an example of a distributed database
  - If that server can resolve the hostname, it does so
  - If not, that server asks another domain name server

15-35

Notes

Computer Science
Illuminated
SECOND EDITION
Nell Dale • John Lewis

Chapter 16
The World Wide Web

Chapter Goals

- Compare and contrast the Internet and the World Wide Web
- Describe general Web processing
- Write basic HTML documents
- Describe several specific HTML tags and their purposes

16-2

Chapter Goals

- Describe the processing of Java applets and Java server pages
- Compare and contrast HTML and XML
- Define basic XML documents and their corresponding DTDs
- Explain how XML documents are viewed

16-3

Notes

The World Wide Web

- **The Web** An infrastructure of distributed information combined with software that uses networks as a vehicle to exchange that information

- **Web page** A document that contains or references various kinds of data, such as text, images, graphics, and programs

- **Links** A connection between one web page and another that can be used "move around" as desired

16-4

The World Wide Web

- **Website** A collection of related web pages

- The Internet makes the communication possible, but the Web makes that communication easy, more productive, and more enjoyable

16-5

Search Engines

- Search Engine A website that helps you find other websites
  - For example, Yahoo and Google are search engines
  - You enter keywords and the search engine produces a list if links to potentially useful sites

- There are two types of searches
  - Keyword searches
  - Concept-based searches

16-6

Instant Messaging

- **Instant messaging** (IM) An application that allows people to send and receive messages in real time
  - Both sender and receiver must have an IM running
  - Most IM applications use a proprietary protocol that dictates the precise format and structure of the messages that are sent across the network to the receiver.
  - Instant messages are not secure

16-7

Cookies

- **Cookie** A small text file that a web server stores on your local computer's hard disk
  - A cookie contains information about your visit to the site
  - Cookies can be used
    - to determine number of unique visitors to the site
    - to customize the site for your future visits
    - to implement shopping carts that can be maintained from visit to visit
  - Cookies are not dangerous

16-8

Web Browser

- **Browser** A software tool that issues the request for the web page we want and displays it when it arrives
- We often talk about "visiting" a website, as if we were going there
  - In truth, we actually specify the information we want, and it is brought to us
  - The concept of visiting a site is understandable in that we often don't know what's at a particular site until we "go to it" and see

16-9

Notes

Web Browser

- **Web server** The computer that is set up to respond to web requests

- **Web address** The core part of a **Uniform Resource Locator**, or **URL**, which uniquely identifies the page you want out of all of the pages stored anywhere in the world

16-10

Web Browser

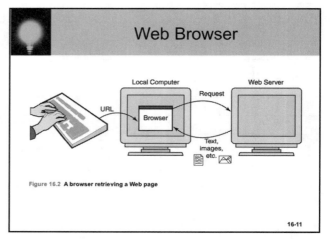

Figure 16.2 **A browser retrieving a Web page**

16-11

HTML

- Web pages are created (or built) using a language called the **Hypertext Markup Language,** or **HTML**

- The term **markup language** comes from the fact that the primary elements of the language take the form of **tags** that we insert into a document to annotate the information stored there

16-12

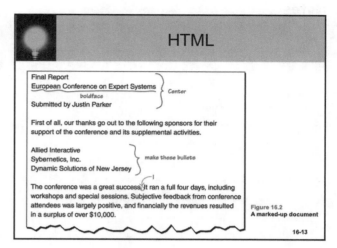

Figure 16.2
A marked-up document

16-13

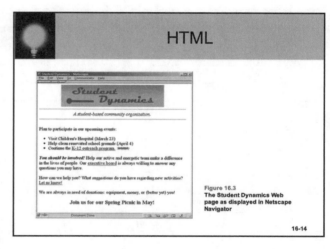

Figure 16.3
The Student Dynamics Web page as displayed in Netscape Navigator

16-14

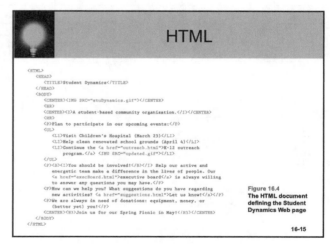

Figure 16.4
The HTML document defining the Student Dynamics Web page

16-15

Notes

HTML

- Tags are enclosed in angle brackets (<. . . >)
- Words such as HEAD, TITLE, and BODY are called elements and specify the type of the tag
- Tags are often used in pairs, with a start tag such as <BODY> and a corresponding end tag with a / before the element name, such as </BODY>

16-16

HTML

- The browser determines how the page should be displayed based on the tags
- The browser
  - Ignores the way we format the HTML document using carriage returns, extra spaces, and blank lines
  - Takes into account the width and height of the browser window
  - Reformats the contents to fit your browser window

16-17

Basic HTML Formatting

- The paragraph tags (<P> . . . </P>) specify text that should be treated as a separate paragraph
- The center tags (<CENTER> . . . </CENTER>) indicate that the enclosed information should be centered in the browser window

16-18

Basic HTML Formatting

- The B, I, and U elements are used to indicate that the enclosed text should be bold, italic, or underlined, respectively

- The <HR> tag inserts a horizontal rule (that is, a line) across the page

16-19

Basic HTML Formatting

- We often have cause to display a list of items

  The UL element stands for an unordered list, and the LI element represents a list item

- Several elements are used to define headings in a document

  There are six predefined heading elements defined in HTML: H1, H2, H3, H4, H5, and H6

16-20

Images and Links

- Many tags can contain attributes that indicate additional details about the information or how the enclosed information should be displayed

  – An image can be incorporated into a web page using the IMG element, which takes an attribute that identifies the image file to display

  – <IMG SRC = "myPicture.gif">

16-21

Images and Links (cont.)

- A link is specified using the element A, which stands for anchor

- The tag includes an attribute called HREF that specifies the URL of the destination document.

For example

```
<A HREF = "http://duke.csc.villanova.edu/docs/">
    Documentation Central!</A>
```

16-22

Interactive Web Pages

- When HTML was first developed, there was no way to interact with the information and pictures presented in a web page

- As users have clamored for a more dynamic web, new technologies were developed to accommodate these requests

- Many of the new ideas were offshoots of the newly developed Java programming language

16-23

Java Applets

- **Java applet** A program that is designed to be embedded into an HTML document and transferred over the Web to someone who wants to run the program

  An applet is embedded into an HTML document using the APPLET tag

  ```
  <APPLET code="MyApplet.class" width=250
      height=150 ></APPLET>
  ```

16-24

Java Applets

- A browser has a built-in interpreter that executes the applet, allowing the user to interact with it.
  - Consider the difficulties inherent in this situation
  - How can we execute a program that was written on one type of computer on possibly many other types of computers?

16-25

Java Applets

- Java programs are compiled into Bytecode, a low-level representation of a program that is not the machine code for any particular type of CPU

- Java applets are restricted as to what they can do
  - The Java language has a carefully constructed security model
  - An applet, for instance, cannot access any local files or change any system settings

16-26

Java Server Pages

- A Java Server Page, or JSP, is a web page that has **JSP scriptlets** embedded in them

- Scriptlet   A small piece of executable code intertwined among regular HTML content

16-27

Java Server Pages

- A JSP scriptlet is encased in special tags beginning with <% and ending with %>

- Imagine JSP scriptlets as having the expressive power of a full programming language

```
<H3>
<%
out.println ("hello there");
%>
</H3>
```

Page 488

16-28

Java Server Pages

- Note that JSPs are executed on the server side where the web page resides

- By the time it arrives at your computer, all active processing has taken place, producing a static (though dynamically created) web page

- JSPs are particularly good for coordinating the interaction between a web page and an underlying database

16-29

XML

- HTML has a predefined set of tags and each tag has its own meaning

- There is nothing about HTML tags that describes the true content of a document

- The **Extensible Markup Language,** or **XML,** allows the creator of a document to describe its contents by defining his or her own set of tags

16-30

XML

- **Metalanguage** A language for talking about, or defining, other languages
- XML is a metalanguage

16-31

XML

```
<?xml version="1.0" ?>
<!DOCTYPE books SYSTEM "books.dtd">
<books>
<book>
<title>The Hobbit</title>
<authors>
  <author>J.R.R. Tolkien</author>
</authors>
<publisher>Ballantine</publisher>
<pages>287</pages>
<isbn>0-345-27257-9</isbn>
<price currency="USD">7.95</price>
</book>
<book>
<title>A Beginner's Guide to Bass Fishing</title>
<authors>
  <author>J. T. Angler</author>
  <author>Ross G. Clearwater</author>
</authors>
<publisher>Quantas Publishing</publisher>
<pages>750</pages>
<isbn>0-781-40211-7</isbn>
<price currency="USD">24.00</price>
</book>
</books>
```

- Like HTML, an XML document is made up of tagged data

Figure 16.5 **An XLML document containing data about books**

16-32

XML

- **Document Type Definition (DTD)** A specification of the organization of the document
- The structure of a particular XML document is described by its corresponding DTD document

```
<!ELEMENT books (book*) >
<!ELEMENT book (title, authors, publisher, pages, isbn, price)>
<!ELEMENT authors (author+)>
<!ELEMENT title (#PCDATA)>
<!ELEMENT author (#PCDATA)>
<!ELEMENT publisher (#PCDATA)>
<!ELEMENT pages (#PCDATA)>
<!ELEMENT isbn (#PCDATA)>
<!ELEMENT price (#PCDATA)>
<!ATTLIST price currency CDATA #REQUIRED>
```

Figure 16.6 **The DTD document corresponding to the XML books document** 16-33

Notes

_____

_____

_____

_____

_____

_____

_____

_____

_____

_____

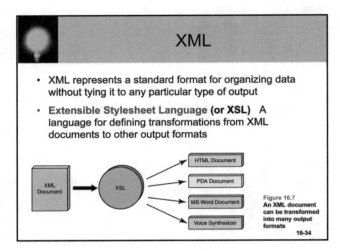

XML

- XML represents a standard format for organizing data without tying it to any particular type of output

- **Extensible Stylesheet Language (or XSL)** A language for defining transformations from XML documents to other output formats

Figure 16.7
An XML document can be transformed into many output formats

16-34

Chapter 17: Limitations of Computing

Notes

Computer Science Illuminated
SECOND EDITION
Nell Dale • John Lewis

Chapter 17
Limitations of Computing

Chapter Goals

- Describe the limits that the hardware places on the solution to computing problems

- Discuss how the finiteness of the computer impacts the solutions to numeric problems

- Discuss ways to ensure that errors in data transmission are detected

- Describe the limits that the software places on the solutions to computing problems

17-2

Chapter Goals

- Discuss ways to build better software

- Describe the limits inherent in computable problems themselves

- Discuss the continuum of problem complexity from problems in Class P to problems that are unsolvable

17-3

Notes

Limits on Arithmetic

- There are limitations imposed by the hardware on the representations of both integer numbers and real numbers

  – If the word length is 32 bits, the range of integer numbers that can be represented is 22,147,483,648 to 2,147,483,647

  – There are software solutions, however, that allow programs to overcome these limitations

  – For example, we could represent a very large number as a list of smaller numbers

17-4

Limits on Arithmetic

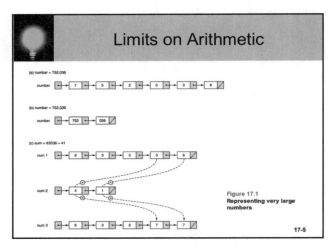

Figure 17.1
Representing very large numbers

17-5

Limits on Arithmetic

Real numbers are stored as an integer along with information showing the location of the radix point

- Let's assume that we have a computer in which each memory location is the same size and is divided into a sign plus five decimal digits

- When a real variable is declared or a real constant is defined, the number stored there has both a whole number part and a fractional part

17-6

Notes

Limits on Arithmetic

- The range of the numbers we can represent with five digits is 299,999 through +99,999:

−	9	9	9	9	9	Largest negative number
+	0	0	0	0	0	Zero
+	9	9	9	9	9	Largest positive number

Page 505

17-7

Limits on Arithmetic

- The precision (the maximum number of digits that can be represented) is five digits, and each number within that range can be represented exactly
- What happens if we allow one of these digits (let's say the leftmost one, in red) to represent an exponent?
- For example

| + | 3 | 5 | 3 | 4 | 2 | Page 505 |

- represents the number +2.345 * 10³

17-8

Limits on Arithmetic

- The range of numbers we can now represent is much larger:

-9,999 * 109 to +9,999 * 109
or
29,999,000,000,000 to +9,999,000,000,000

- We can represent only four **significant digits**

17-9

Limits on Arithmetic

- The four leftmost digits are correct, and the balance of the digits are assumed to be zero

- We lose the rightmost, or *least significant*, digits

Number	Sign	Exp.					Value
+99,999	+	1	9	9	9	9	+99,990
−999,999	−	2	9	9	9	9	−999,900
+1,000,000	+	3	1	0	0	0	+1,000,000
−4,932,416	−	3	4	9	3	2	−4,932,000

Page 505   17-10

Limits on Arithmetic

- To extend our coding scheme to represent real numbers, we need to be able to represent negative exponents.

- For example

$$4{,}394 * 10^{-2} = 43.94$$
or
$$22 * 10^{-4} = 0.0022$$

17-11

Limits on Arithmetic

- Add a sign to the left of it to be the sign of the number itself

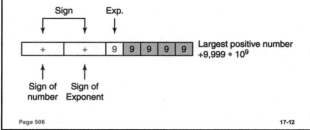

Page 506   17-12

Notes

Limits on Arithmetic

$$
\begin{array}{ll}
(y) & 1325000 * 10^0 \\
(z) & \underline{5424 * 10^0} \\
& 1330424 * 10^0 = 1330 * 10^3 \text{ (truncated to four} \\
& \hspace{8.5em} \text{digits)} \\[1em]
(y + z) & 1330 * 10^3 \\
(x) & \underline{-1324 * 10^3} \\
& 6 * 10^3 = 6000 * 10^0 = x + (y + z)
\end{array}
$$

- This is called **representational error** or **round-off error**

17-13

Limits on Arithmetic

- In addition to representational errors, there are two other problems to watch out for in floating-point arithmetic: *underflow* and *overflow*

  - **Underflow** The condition that arises when the absolute value of a calculation gets too small to be represented

  - **Overflow** The condition that arises when the absolute value of a calculation gets too large to be represented

17-14

Limits on Arithmetic

- **Cancellation error** Another type of error that can happen with floating-point numbers

  This error happens when numbers of widely differing magnitudes are added or subtracted

17-15

Notes

Limits on Arithmetic

$(1 + 0.00001234 - 1) = 0.00001234$

$$
\begin{array}{r}
100000000 * 10^{-8} \\
+ \ 1234 * 10^{-8} \\
\hline
100001234 * 10^{-8}
\end{array}
$$

- With four-digit accuracy, this becomes $1000 * 10^{-3}$.
- Now the computer subtracts 1:

$$
\begin{array}{r}
1000 * 10^{-3} \\
- \ 1000 * 10^{-3} \\
\hline
0
\end{array}
$$

- The result is 0, not .00001234

17-16

Limits on Communications

- Error-detecting codes determine that an error has occurred during the transmission of data and then alert the system

- Error-correcting codes not only determine that an error has occurred but try to determine the correct value actually

17-17

Limits on Communications

- Parity bits are used to detect that an error has occurred between the storing and retrieving of a byte or the sending and receiving of a byte

    Parity bit An extra bit that is associated with each byte, used to ensure that the number of 1 bits in a 9-bit value (byte plus parity bit) is odd (or even) across all bytes

17-18

Limits on Communications

- *Odd parity* requires the number of 1s in a byte plus parity bit to be odd

  For example
  - If a byte contains the pattern 11001100, the parity bit would be 1, thus giving an odd number of 1s
  - If the pattern were 11110001, the parity bit would be 0, giving an odd number of 1s

- *Even parity* uses the same scheme, but the number of 1 bits must be even

17-19

Limits on Communications

- Check digits
  - A software variation of the same scheme is to sum the individual digits of a number, and then store the unit's digit of that sum with the number
  - For example, given the number 34376, the sum of the digits is 23, so the number would be stored as 34376–3

- Error-correcting codes
  - If enough information about a byte or number is kept, it is possible to deduce what an incorrect bit or digit must be

17-20

Complexity of Software

- Commercial software contains errors
  - The problem is *complexity*
  - Software testing can demonstrate the presence of bugs but *cannot demonstrate their absence*
    - As we find problems and fix them, we raise our confidence that the software performs as it should
    - But we can never guarantee that all bugs have been removed

17-21

Notes

Software Engineering

- In Chapter 6, we outlined three stages of computer problem solving
  - Develop the algorithm
  - Implement the algorithm
  - Maintain the program
- When we move from small, well-defined tasks to large software projects, we need to add two extra layers on top of these: *Software requirements* and *specifications*

17-22

Software Engineering

- **Software requirements** Broad, but precise, statements outlining what is to be provided by the software product
- **Software specifications** A detailed description of the function, inputs, processing, outputs, and special features of a software product

17-23

Software Engineering

- A guideline for the number of errors per lines of code that can be expected
  - Standard software: 25 bugs per 1,000 lines of program
  - Good software: 2 errors per 1,000 lines
  - Space Shuttle software: < 1 error per 10,000 lines

17-24

Formal Verification

- The verification of program correctness, independent of data testing, is an important area of theoretical computer science research

- Formal methods have been used successfully in verifying the correctness of computer chips

- It is hoped that success with formal verification techniques at the hardware level can lead eventually to success at the software level

17-25

Notorious Software Errors

- AT&T Down for Nine Hours
  - In January of 1990, AT&T's long-distance telephone network came to a screeching halt for nine hours, because of a software error in an upgrade to the electronic switching systems

17-26

Notorious Software Errors

- Therac-25
  - Between June 1985 and January 1987, six known accidents involved massive overdoses by the Therac-25, leading to deaths and serious injuries
  - There was only a single coding error, but tracking down the error exposed that the whole design was seriously flawed

17-27

Notes

Notorious Software Errors

- Mariner 1 Venus Probe

  This probe, launched in July of 1962, veered off course almost immediately and had to be destroyed

  The problem was traced to the following line of Fortran code:

  ```
  DO 5 K = 1. 3
  ```

  The period should have been a comma.

  An $18.5 million space exploration vehicle was lost because of this typographical error

17-28

Big-O Analysis

- A function of the size of the input to the operation (for instance, the number of elements in the list to be summed)

- We can express an approximation of this function using a mathematical notation called order of magnitude, or **Big-O notation**

17-29

Big-O Analysis

$$f(N) = N^4 + 100N^2 + 10N + 50$$

- Then $f(N)$ is of order N^4—or, in Big-O notation, $O(N^4)$.

- For large values of N, N^4 is so much larger than 50, $10N$, or even $100 \, N^2$ that we can ignore these other terms

17-30

Notes

Big-O Analysis

- **Common Orders of Magnitude**
  - *O(1) is called bounded time*
    - Assigning a value to the *i*th element in an array of *N* elements
  - *O(log₂N) is called logarithmic time*
    - Algorithms that successively cut the amount of data to be processed in half at each step typically fall into this category
    - Finding a value in a list of sorted elements using the binary search algorithm is $O(log_2N)$

17-31

Big-O Analysis

- *O(N) is called linear is called linear time*
  - Printing all the elements in a list of *N* elements is *O(N)*
- *O(N log₂N)*
  - Algorithms of this type typically involve applying a logarithmic algorithm *N* times
  - The better sorting algorithms, such as Quicksort, Heapsort, and Mergesort, have $N \log_2N$ complexity

17-32

Big-O Analysis

- *O(N²) is called quadratic time*
  - Algorithms of this type typically involve applying a linear algorithm *N* times. Most simple sorting algorithms are *O(N²)* algorithms
- *O(2ᴺ) is called exponential time*

17-33

Big-O Analysis

– *O(n!)* is called factorial time

- The traveling salesperson graph algorithm is a factorial time algorithm

- Algorithms whose order of magnitude can be expressed as a polynomial in the size of the problem are called polynomial-time algorithms

- All polynomial-time algorithms are defined as being in Class P

17-34

Big-O Analysis

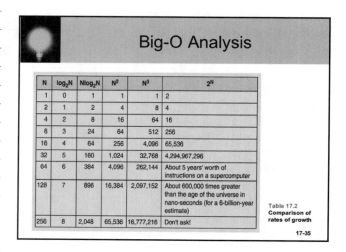

N	$\log_2 N$	$N\log_2 N$	N^2	N^3	2^N
1	0	1	1	1	2
2	1	2	4	8	4
4	2	8	16	64	16
8	3	24	64	512	256
16	4	64	256	4,096	65,536
32	5	160	1,024	32,768	4,294,967,296
64	6	384	4,096	262,144	About 5 years' worth of instructions on a supercomputer
128	7	896	16,384	2,097,152	About 600,000 times greater than the age of the universe in nano-seconds (for a 6-billion-year estimate)
256	8	2,048	65,536	16,777,216	Don't ask!

Table 17.2
Comparison of rates of growth

17-35

Big-O Analysis

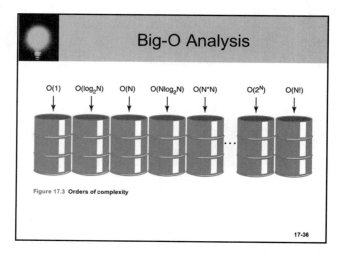

$O(1)$ $O(\log_2 N)$ $O(N)$ $O(N\log_2 N)$ $O(N*N)$ $O(2^N)$ $O(N!)$

Figure 17.3 Orders of complexity

17-36

Turing Machines

- Alan Turing developed the concept of a computing machine in the 1930s

- A Turing machine, as his model became known, consists of a control unit with a read/write head that can read and write symbols on an infinite tape

17-37

Turing Machines

- Why is such a simple machine (model) of any importance?

  – It is widely accepted that *anything that is intuitively computable can be computed by a Turing machine*

  – If we can find a problem for which a Turing-machine solution can be proven not to exist, then the problem must be unsolvable

Figure 17.4 **Turing machine processing**   17-38

Halting Problem

- It is not always obvious that a computation (program) halts

- The **Halting problem:** Given a program and an input to the program, determine if the program will eventually stop with this input

- This problem is unsolvable

17-39

Notes

Halting Problem

- Assume that there exists a Turing-machine program, called **SolvesHaltingProblem** that determines for any program **Example** and input **SampleData** whether program **Example** halts given input **SampleData**

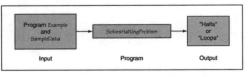

Figure 17.5 **Proposed program for solving the Halting problem**

17-40

Halting Problem

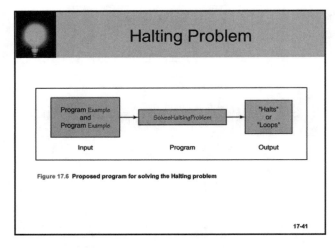

Figure 17.6 **Proposed program for solving the Halting problem**

17-41

Halting Problem

- Now let's construct a new program, **NewProgram,** that takes program **Example** as both program and data and uses the algorithm from **SolvesHaltingProblem** to write "Halts" if **Example** halts and "Loops" if it does not halt

- Let's now apply program **SolvesHaltingProblem** to **NewProgram,** using **NewProgram** as data

  - If **SolvesHaltingProblem** prints "Halts", program **NewProgram** goes into an infinite loop

  - If **SolvesHaltingProblem** prints "Loops", program **NewProgram** prints "Halts" and stops

  - In either case, **SolvesHaltingProblem** gives the wrong answer

17-42

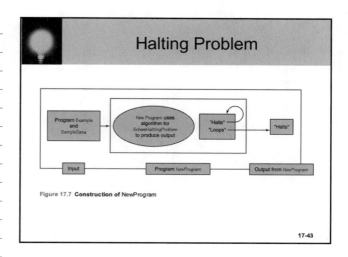

Halting Problem

Figure 17.7 **Construction of** NewProgram

17-43

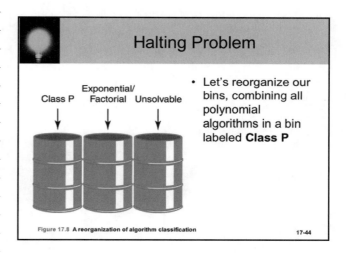

Halting Problem

Class P   Exponential/Factorial   Unsolvable

- Let's reorganize our bins, combining all polynomial algorithms in a bin labeled **Class P**

Figure 17.8 **A reorganization of algorithm classification**

17-44

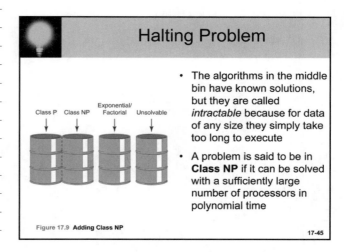

Halting Problem

Class P   Class NP   Exponential/Factorial   Unsolvable

- The algorithms in the middle bin have known solutions, but they are called *intractable* because for data of any size they simply take too long to execute

- A problem is said to be in **Class NP** if it can be solved with a sufficiently large number of processors in polynomial time

Figure 17.9 **Adding Class NP**

17-45